The Road from Kharkiv:
A Journey of Pain in Pursuit of
Love, God and Sense
Katheryna Fedorova
ISBN: 978-1-914933-58-5

Published By: -

i2i

PUBLISHING

i2i Publishing. Manchester.
www.i2i.publishing.co.uk

My Dear Reader,
I have written this book for you.
You are an amazing person and can achieve any
goals, realise any dreams and find happiness.
You were the one who raised my confidence
and made me tenacious with my writing.
You prevented me from giving up.
I devote my book, my love, my heart to you!
Forever yours,
Katheryna Fedorova

Acknowledgements

First and foremost, praise and thanks to God, for His shower of blessings over me during the writing of this book.

Certainly, there are countless people I would like to thank for their help throughout my life. Without them, I would not be who I am or would have done what I am now doing.

I would like to acknowledge and thank those who had the greatest impact on the creation of this book.

My English teacher Elina Shevchenko, who believed in me while I was writing this book, always pushing and inspiring me. When I felt low and hesitant, she wrote to me providing her support, encouraging me to keep going. She stood by me during every struggle and all my doubts.

I am eternally grateful to my friend, Steve Cushing, a much-published British writer, for his help. After reading my book, he reacted very positively. He shared his experience and gave me wise recommendations. He is the one who played a significant role in introducing the idea of this book to the world.

Special thanks to Lionel Ross, my publisher and the proprietor of i2i Publishing and Mark Cripps, my editor. They realised my dream and gave me a chance to present my book to the world. I will never forget the day when Lionel sent me a letter with his final decision, a decision which changed my life dramatically and made me supremely happy. It has been a great pleasure to work with his team.

My husband Maxim and my three beloved children Misha, Annya and Lev - you are my continuous source of love and inspiration. Without your unconditional support, this book never would have come into being.

My grandmother, who raised me up and believed in my success is not alive now but continues looking after me from above. I must also thank my mum and my aunt Toma; they always wish me the best.

In addition, I must thank my new Austrian friends, Martha and Franz, Gerhard and Octavia, Jacqueline and Frederick, Katja and a lot of other wonderful people living in Podersdorf. You have surrounded me with love and care and given me the strength and energy to write.

Special thanks to the people who gave us shelter during our journey from Ukraine, especially Alex, our angel from Romania who covered us with his wings and gave us lavishly of what we needed.

Also, I want to say thank you to my dear friends Tanja, Olya, and Yana who are always next to me and on whom I can rely for their support.

I am a happy person as I do not have enemies, only good friends - the people I love. This book is my first book in English and my fourth overall. Every time I finish a new book, I feel incredible, like after the birth of a new child.

I asked myself many times why I had arrived in Austria and now I know the answer: I am here in order to have written this book.

So, thank you, Austria, for providing the conditions to make my dream come true.

Contents

Prologue

A Day Before

Life is Beautiful

It was a lovely morning. I woke up with a smile on my face. I was full of positive thoughts and joyful energy. 'What a wonderful day,' I thought. I went to the kitchen to cook breakfast for my three children and my husband, Maxim. I always prepared something delicious for them in the morning. Every day was different: pancakes, sandwiches, curd cakes, omelette, cookies or even pies. That day, I cooked some pancakes with jam and honey.

Everyone was sitting in the kitchen and eating breakfast. We were discussing our plans for the day. The atmosphere in the room was warm and friendly. I was looking at my children and felt tiptoes inside my heart. 'How I adore it when my family is together,' I thought and smiled contentedly.

Later, my older son Misha and daughter Annya went to school, and Maxim took my youngest, Lev to a nanny. I closed the door and sighed with happiness. Time alone in the flat … I always adored these happy moments of silence and solitude. I took a mug of tea and went to the living room to start my work. I am an English teacher and I was teaching students online.

Actually, it was not my only profession. My life was always so active and full of contrast. That day after lessons, I went to the city centre to do a photo session for a lovely couple and their little one-year-old baby. Photography was my inspirational hobby, my vital air and my endless love. This magic process made me alive and happy.

When I finished my shoot, I met with a girl who wanted to buy my books and my metaphoric cards. My heart was always elated when people called me to get something I had created. I felt wonderfully alive.

After that, I had a very responsible event for children in the boarding school. I played my transformational game 'Purpose of Life' for them. It was my volunteer job and I adored spending time with the children there. They had a hard childhood, most of them did not have parents. But their hearts were angelic and they always looked forward to my arrival. It made me do more and more. My dream was to inspire them, give them a trigger to start changing their life and achieve success. When they spoke their mind and started dreaming about their future, my soul always took flight.

During the game, one teenager said that he had never received a gift in his life. This touched my heart deeply. Immediately, a plan developed in my head. I ran to the nearest shop and bought him a game called 'Jango'.

I came back to the boarding school and gave it to him and said, "This is your first present. But I am sure you will get a lot of gifts in your life. I hope you will also help people and make them happier. I believe in you."

"Yes, I will," he answered and looked at me with such a deep and wise gaze. That moment stuck in my memory for a long time after. He did not say a lot but his eyes said everything. I went to the bus station thinking about this sensitive moment and smiled. I felt a glimmer of happiness.

After all these activities, I was a bit tired going to my own English school. In the evening, I was going to run an English psychological speaking club.

I remember my mood exactly. I was full of kindness and happiness. My heart leaped for joy. The weather was magic. It was snowing but it was not very cold and there was no wind and mud. It was a perfect evening in my favourite city, Kharkiv. I raised my head and looked up at the sky, closed my eyes and tried to catch snowflakes with my mouth. I wanted to finish a wonderful day with one more kind act. I saw a woman who was selling tulips. 'Wow, tulips in winter! What a surprise,' I thought and went up to her.

"Can I buy all the flowers?" I asked.

"Really? I have twenty-one flowers. Are you sure?" she replied.

"Yes," I said and gave her the money.

I wanted to present these flowers to the girls at the speaking club. At that moment, I did not give a thought to the fact that in this way, I would not earn any money from the lesson. But I wanted to make them happy. In addition, the topic of our speaking club was self-confidence. What could raise self-confidence better for women? Yes, of course, flowers.

When I arrived at the office, I saw a woman with the same flowers. It was a miracle. She had bought the same tulips from the same woman near the underground like me, but before me.

"Kate, these flowers are for you. I saw this charming bunch and wanted to make you happy," she said.

I smiled and gave her the same bunch. Gratitude flowed through me.

"Exchange," I said with a smile.

We laughed and hugged emotionally.

The lesson was great. People were participating in the discussion very actively and it seemed to me that the experience was really raising their self-confidence and making them a bit more joyful. In the end, everyone went home with flowers and with happiness glowing inside them. Their eyes were sparkling with exhilaration and it raised my spirit too.

After the lesson, my friend Yana came to me and gave me a packet of small pies filled with meat and cottage cheese. She looked so softly at me and said, "Kate, this is for you. You are probably hungry now."

"Thank you, my dear. It is so kind of you," I answered and hugged her.

Her pies were a sign of her caring about me, an expression of her love and friendship.

We smiled together and ate the pies while thinking that we were happy to be friends and could always support each other. Then, I went home to my family.

I ran home under an amazing shower of snow with a bunch of flowers and unspeakable feelings inside. 'Life is beautiful!' I was repeating in my soul. My heart was singing. I was treasuring every moment.

At home, my children and Maxim were waiting for me. I cooked a tasty dinner and we watched an interesting comedy. I did not want this day to finish. It was one of the best days.

I spent some time in the kids' room. We were playing board games and we chatted. Then, we lay in the bed all together. I was between Misha and Annya.

I said, "We are like a hot dog together. I am a sausage and you are my lovely buns."

They laughed and kissed me before I left their room.

Very soon, my children were sleeping peacefully in their beds and my husband and I were locked in each other's passionate embraces. We fell asleep in each other's arms. I could not think of a time I had ever been happier.

Chapter 1

The Fateful Morning

Life is a long lesson in humility
— *James M. Barrie*

It was about five o'clock. Suddenly, I woke up. A loud noise, a shout from my Annya, and one from Maxim pronounced one painful word which pierced my heart: WAR.

It is impossible to forget this moment. It changed our calm and peaceful life, forever.

Quickly, I jumped from my bed and ran towards the kids' room. I grabbed Annya from the bed and Misha followed us. We all sat on the floor in the corridor. I hugged Annya who was trembling and crying quietly and squeezed Misha's hand. Maxim held Lev, who was just one year old. He was completely unaware of what was happening. We stayed in the hall listening to the sounds of bombs but could not come to terms with our new reality. We could not believe what was happening. It seemed like a bad dream. Perhaps we were still sleeping. We wanted to believe that it was something temporary or that we had just misheard, a simple noise somewhere far-far-away. But when I went into the kitchen and looked through the window, I could see a big explosion near our house. My heart skipped a beat. It was obvious that the war had already started.

My husband came up to me and read the news on the phone, "Putin announced the war against Ukraine," he said. There were no doubts about what had just begun and we could not change the situation.

The war begins. Buildings near us are bombed.

All day, we heard the noise of endless shelling of our city. Annya was very scared. She asked me to read a prayer to her, and I read Psalm 90. She read the prayer on the floor non-stop, asking God to help and to protect us. It was quite frightening to see how a seven-year-old girl, happy a few hours before, was now crying on the floor and reading a Psalm. She asked me numerous questions, "Mum, why does somebody want to kill us?" I was incapable of giving her any appropriate answer.

Staying in the corridor, we tried to gather our thoughts, and reflected on our next steps. We were in a dangerous place. Our house was near the motorway and the Russian border. We understood that we were in the middle of everything.

Continuing to live on the ninth floor of our apartment block was quite risky. So, we packed all our necessities and decided to go to our office, the private English school which we had been building up from scratch for more than ten years, a base which now would become a place of survival for us. We assumed that it was a safer place because it was on the first floor and near the underground. Having considered the benefits of changing our location, we set off.

In the early morning, under continuous shelling, we walked together towards the school. We were loaded up with a lot of heavy bags, dragging a pram with a crying baby. Maxim and I were trying to hide our fear from the children. We pretended to be brave and calm, but inside us, our hearts were crying and asking for help.

Crossing the path near the supermarket, Misha suddenly shouted, "Mum, a dead raven has fallen down in front of me!"

At first, I did not understand what he meant, but soon, I was looking at the dead bird covered in blood. I had a horrible feeling ... I do not believe in superstitions but at that moment, I thought that it was not a good sign for us. The poor bird, what had happened to it? People were fighting, and nature was suffering. Why should animals die from people's senseless fighting?

Soon, we arrived at our school. When we went inside, I thought that we should stay for a while. It was the second time I received a message deep from inside of me. The first time was at home, when I suggested moving to a safer place. Before that, I thought that all my messages were simply gut feelings, but soon these messages became more and more accurate and detailed. I started to believe in God's help.

After that, our life in the school started. It seemed unreal, as if we were acting in a film. The kids slept on the chairs, Maxim was on the floor and I slept on the massage bed which I had bought just a month before the war. I had completed a course with a school of massage and organised a little room in our school for doing my massage job. Also, I had been providing my transformational games for people there as a coach and a psychologist. This room was designed as a dream place for realising my big mission, that of helping people. But now, as well as becoming the place I was going to sleep in, it had become my secret place for hiding and praying to God in order to save our lives.

Every day, we heard the sound of bombing and shooting. It was extremely difficult to switch our attention from these sounds to habitual life such as cooking, cleaning, and sleeping.

We closed our windows tightly, so we didn't see the world outside. We were sitting in one room together like in a bunker, hoping another bomb would not explode somewhere close. Every hour, the war was intensifying more and more and also, our feelings of fear were increasing. Our hearts started beating faster and faster. We could not know how long it would last nor if we would be alive after the nightmare ended.

During our stay in the school, my friend Yana texted me and called me often. We were worried about each other. Every time, she shouted to me, "RUN TO THE CELLAR!" But we could not go there. There was not enough room for our big family, so we were on the floor near the walls in the school. We prayed.

Besides our fear, we had one more terrible problem, a lack of food. We were a group of five people and all we had was some bread, a little water and something for Lev, who needed special baby food. On the third day, we almost ran out of food and I made up my mind to go home to get some.

I remember clearly that I woke up at eight and got a message inside of me, 'Go now!'. Maxim was against it, and he tried to dissuade me, explaining that it was very dangerous outside and better to wait. I felt that it was now or never. Furthermore, I wanted to fetch our cat, Tishka, from the flat. He had been alone there all of this time. After three days, he could be dying without food. I had to save him.

I was packed as though I was going hiking, with a huge rucksack and some bags in my hands. At nine o'clock in the morning, I left our school and very soon, approached the main road near the underground which was closed for safety measures. The way to the house was very dangerous. The most difficult part was going across two wide roads, where tanks were passing from time to time. The streets were silent at that moment. It seemed that everyone was hiding in anticipation of something bad happening. I ran very quickly across the road, trying to reach a safer place on the other side as soon as possible.

I did it! My heart was jumping like crazy. I kept moving while repeating the same words, "God, if you need me, if my life is still important, I will be alive." I mumbled these words like a prayer without stopping. It helped me very much, because I relied on God's judgement. I trusted him and knew that he wanted the best for me.

Twenty minutes later, I reached our building. I was so happy to see it. The elevator did not work, so I went up to the ninth floor using the stairs. The building was as quiet as a tomb. At last, I opened the door to our flat and I saw our cat, Tishka. He was happy to see me and I read exactly in his eyes one phrase, 'Thank you.'

I had limited time, so I ran quickly around the flat packing everything in the bags: food, whatever I thought would be useful, the cat's equipment and his food too. I stopped in our bedroom and cried. I looked at our bed, shirts, pillows and everything else we had left. I recalled how we had been sleeping calmly and happily there without any premonitions. I wanted to get the time back, but I couldn't. It was God's plan and we had to follow it.

Tishka. Grateful to be saved.
Now, he was coming with us.

Looking at the time on the telephone, I rushed to the hall. I quickly put Tishka into his cage and hung all the bags on my shoulders. I was ready to go. I was burdened down with many bags. I felt as if my knees were going to give way. It was all too heavy. But I had to go and bring food to my family.

While I was going back, I stopped every two minutes. Tishka was crying loudly; he could not know what was going on outside. The situation was intense and dangerous. I could hear that in front of me, there was fighting. But I had to get back to my family, I did not have any other choice. So, I summoned my courage and kept going as confidently as I could.

I stopped to check my phone and suddenly heard, "Stupid fool. Throw your phone away. Run. Quickly!"

I saw a Ukrainian military man behind the tree. He pointed me towards the underground. I ran towards it but my energy was almost gone. Everything was so heavy that I wanted to lay on the ground and not move. I did not understand what helped me to go further and move so fast but in a few more minutes, I reached the underground. I was happy that I could hide there. I tried to go inside but the main entrance was closed. Thousands of people were inside, but there was no room for anyone else. I found a little safe place near the door and sat on the floor, covered my face with my hands and started praying. I was stuck. I could not go via the roads and could not go through the underground. I was just one hundred metres away from my family but the way there was blocked.

Near me, there was a man, who could not get into the underground to give food to his family. He noticed how I was frightened and crying and he gave me some tea. We talked and he said that one of the Russian tanks had been attacked nearby and a group of Russians were spreading around the district. Everything was closed for safety reasons.

Another significant problem for me was that something had happened to my voice since the beginning of the war. I had lost it. I imagined that the reason was psychological because of the shock and stress. This meant that I was just whispering very quietly with this man, trying to explain my situation. But even my attempts at talking were painful. Each word or phrase required a lot of effort. He looked very nervous but listened to me patiently.

So near and yet, so far from my family.
Outside the underground station.

I drank tea and continued praying. I imagined what my husband and kids were thinking at that moment; how much they were worried about me. Their mother had not come back ... And the poor cat was meowing all the time.

I said to him, "Tishka, my dear, we are stuck. I do not know how to get back. I am very frightened but I believe God will help us. Just wait and see."

The man came up to me and said that he had decided to find a safer place and was planning to go. I stood up and tried to whisper again, "Don't leave me alone here, please ..."

The man took my bags and said to me, "Can I take you to a nearby house. Do you know anybody living near here?"

"Yes," I whispered to him. I remembered that our son's nanny was living nearby. 'Maybe, she will open the door for me', I thought.

We left the underground and moved very quickly, not turning around. While I was following him, I felt a little bit safer. I got accused before that I was always with my husband and he always protected me. And now, I was behind the man's back and thought that I was under his wings. I trusted him so much at that moment. I believed that God sent him to me.

When we reached our nanny's house, we stopped near her porch. I hugged him very tightly and said, "Thank you very much. I want you and your family to be alive and healthy. I will pray for you."

It was painful to say these words for me, but it was important that I said them. He saved my life.

I knocked at the door and Irina, Lev's nanny, answered. She offered me shelter until I decided what to do next. Tishka was crying very loudly so I asked her to give me some space in the hall and let him out of the cage. She agreed and gave me a plate of hot soup. I ate the soup greedily. It tasted incredible. After several days of not eating well, it was like a fresh gulp of happiness. Suddenly, I felt that I was ill. Perhaps, my problem with my voice was also a result of illness. I was in warm clothes, shivering from the temperature, coughing, stroking the cat and crying, thinking about my poor, hungry children. I had food for them, but I did know how to get to them. I was stuck, just waiting for the right moment. Tishka was on my knees and looking at my face with tenderness and love. It seemed to me he was saying, I am with you. Everything will be okay now.

The best tasting soup.

There were five people in Irina's flat, all sitting in the hall in darkness. They were chatting together and discussing the news.

Suddenly, one lady said, "Maybe, it is time to go, Kate, because soon, it will be more dangerous."

"I will go with her," a young man said. He was Irina's relative, and the future husband of her daughter.

Surprisingly, everyone supported his idea and agreed. Happily, I jumped from the seat, ready to go to my hungry and worried family.

I put Tishka back into his cage and soon left the house with the man. 'Again, a brave man is saving me', I was thinking and looked at him full of gratitude. Thank you, God.

We had to cross the two dangerous roads near the motorway again. We were running like spies, silently and quickly. Our task was not to be noticed by Russians and also by our army because the command was to stay at home while the military operation was on.

The streets were suspiciously quiet. There were no people, no cars … just silence. I followed him. He carried Tishka and also helped me with all my bags. After ten minutes of danger, we were already knocking at the door of our school's bunker.

Maxim opened the shutters anxiously and I saw how happy he was to see me alive. At last, he opened the door and jumped forward to hug me.

"I will never let you go again. Why did you go? Why?" he shouted, nearly crying.

Misha also came to me and hugged me tightly. He did not say anything but I saw everything in his eyes. Annya was standing near us and looking frustrated.

But then she saw the cage with Tishka.

"Mummy. You've brought him. Thank you," she said.

We let Tishka out of the cage. Our school was his first temporary home. He did not know yet how many new homes he would visit and how many trials he would have to go through.

From that day, we continued to stay in the school, waiting for positive change. But the war situation was worsening. The days in our school bunker seemed so long and hard. Soon, we could hear Russian airplanes above us. All their planes were passing by our building because we were very near the border. Our days seemed to be spent on the floor in the corners, waiting and praying. It seemed like a gamble. Maybe, their planes would go past us or maybe, they could drop bombs on our building. We just hoped for the best and that they were flying elsewhere. Every day, it was harder and harder to endure the tension and fear.

At such moments a person usually makes decisions on how to behave: to survive or to do something for people, maybe. My voice was still very quiet but it came back just a little. I thought that it might be my last day in the world. 'How do I want to spend my last day?' I asked myself. Firstly, I sent some money from my account to help the Ukrainian military and also, I gave some money for the injured. Then, I recorded a supportive video for people and uploaded it to Facebook. In the video, I tried to inspire people; to give them my love and care. I felt that I was stronger, so I must help those who were weaker. But it was difficult to say anything. My mouth wanted to pronounce the necessary words, but it sounded very quiet. Nevertheless, I did not give up. Nothing could silence me even though I struggled to say each word. I was speaking Ukrainian. It was my intention to speak my national language, although achieving this was an additional trial. I had been born and brought up in a Russian-speaking part of the country, I had never spoken Ukrainian before. I was one of thousands of Ukrainian people who only spoke Russian.

However, I wanted to be brave in everything, especially my love for my country, a love communicated in this case, literally, through its language.

After having made the decision not simply, to survive, but to be brave, every day, I managed to do something for others, the people of my country. I prayed so passionately for several hours to ask God to save me and help people. I imagined my enemies and how I was giving them my light which destroyed their evil. In my imagination, they were leaving my country and going back to their homes. As they became kinder, they became more big-hearted.

Trying to stay safe. Annya, Misha, Lev and I
sit on the floor against the wall in our school.

I prayed not just to stay alive but also, I wanted to influence the world with my prayer. I felt that I was becoming stronger and decisive.

I chose love not fear.

Soon, we were close to running out of food. We had a few things in storage but we didn't know when we could get new supplies. So, we divided what we did have into meals and then, into portions, eating very little at a time. It was almost impossible to find food. All the shops were empty. There were long queues with people surrounded by all the shooting and explosions. There was general hysteria everywhere. Maxim took many risks going outside trying to find food.

When he was gone, I went crazy picturing bloody scenes in my imagination. It was so frightening to stay alone with the kids. Every time, when he went out, I said goodbye to him and kissed him with tenderness. Each kiss might have turned out to be our last. Who knows? And when he came back alive, I savoured the moment and the extra time I would now have with him.

Once, he went to the shop and the phone connection was out. I called him but there was no signal. A lot of time passed but he did not come back. I was going crazy waiting for him for what seemed like hours.

At last, he answered me and I sighed.

"Kate, I am okay. It was a dangerous situation. The shop where I was standing in a queue for several hours was closed. Another one was empty. I went to the chemist and there, I was able to buy something for us: some kid's food. I think it will be enough for today. I am coming home, my love. Don't worry."

The next day, we were struggling to find food again. We were hungry almost all the time and tried to find ways to get more food. It was so painful to see as your children wanted to eat but had to wait for the next snack or whatever we could find for them.

One night, I was preparing our dinner, which consisted of just a few, small sandwiches. I put together slices of sausage, cheese and bread and added some vegetables. I made about five little sandwiches and went to another room for a few minutes. When I came back, everybody was eating the sandwiches and I saw that mine had been eaten already. I was facing the challenge of going to bed hungry when suddenly, Misha cut his sandwich in half and gave it to me.

"Mum, you will be hungry. This is enough for me," he said, holding out the sandwich.

"Misha, no. I can't. It is okay. Don't worry about me," I replied waving away his offering.

"No, I want to give it to you. For you it is more important," he insisted.

We finished with dinner and I went to my little prayer room and burst into tears. What Misha had done touched my heart very much. This moment of his love and his kindness was far more important than any beautiful words. This was real LOVE. It was a real deed. My son was hungry but gave me his last piece of sandwich.

The days that followed were more and more dangerous and difficult to survive. Every time we went to find some food, we took a big risk. It was so hazardous to go out. Bombs were flying from the sky and you went to the shop and told yourself that you would not die this day, that with luck, you could come back home alive.

We could not get any special food for Lev, so he had to eat the same food as we did. Once, we had dumplings but they were already off. The meat inside smelt suspicious. We boiled them in the electric kettle and put a plate of them on the table. We ate them with disgust. Then suddenly, Lev jumped on the plate. With hungry eyes, he gulped a couple of dumplings. He was too young for such unhealthy food but I could not stop him. He wanted to eat so much. My poor hungry baby ...

My friends from Russia and Donbass wrote to me in the early days of the war. They were worried but at the same time, they believed that it was a special operation and Putin had done the right thing.

This was a terrible trap. These people wanted to care about us, their beloved friends but their belief in the craziness of Putin's ideas was greater. When I replied that the Russian army was killing us, and how we had to flee from the Russian tanks, they did not believe me and did not write after that. I lost hundreds of friends who I had known for more than twenty years. One day had changed everything. It looked like 24 February had broken my friendships, my life and my future dreams.

The Russian attacks became more powerful and dangerous. We had to get used to loud noises all day and night. Every time, we fell asleep hoping to stay alive. Nevertheless, we always said goodbye to each other and thanked each other in case we would not wake up in the morning. I was surprised that my children slept heavily. I could not sleep like them, I was lying in the bed and trembling from every sound. Maybe, they accepted it as their new reality. Soon, I was able to accept it too. I had no choice. The war had already begun and we had to put up with it.

I was drowning in dreams, listening to explosions.

Chapter 2

Escape from Kharkiv

Life is either a daring adventure or nothing at all.
— *Helen Keller*

Suddenly, next morning, I woke up very early. I had one, strong, urgent thought in my head, 'YOU MUST GO'. Something again had whispered inside of me and persuaded me that I needed to take action.

Without hesitating, I got up, woke Maxim and announced, "Today or never!"

Maxim was quite surprised by my persistence and he tried to calm me down. He replied, "Okay, Kate, I agree that we must go to another safer place. But I suppose we should do everything in a well-organized way. Let's go to our flat and collect all our possessions and tomorrow, we will set out. We should do everything without rushing."

"Maybe, you are right," I said agreeing with him but I was still worried, and my heart continued beating nervously. My instinct was telling me to do things immediately. We had been in the school for two weeks. But now it was time to move on.

We started to get together all our possessions from the school. The children also helped us, packing everything in bags. We were in a rush, and kept our ears peeled for the alarm. At any time, there could be a big explosion. We wanted to leave our school at a quiet time.

As well as our possessions, I begged Maxim to take my newly published books with us. They had been printed only recently. For me, it was painful to leave them to fade in the school. I had written them for people to make their lives better and more fulfilling. The books were part of me, a result of my hard work over many years. He agreed but hesitantly, as we had too little room in our car. Taking the books would mean leaving other things. It was so hard to decide what to take and what to leave behind. We had to make ruthless decisions about our priorities, deciding what was vital and what was not.

We were ready to go. Our car was packed. We closed the doors and checked the windows. I leaned towards the wall of the school and quietly whispered, "I love you so much, my office. I have been building you up for so long and with care. Now, I have to leave you. Sorry, my dear. I promise, I will come back soon. Please, be brave and stay intact." Finally, I kissed the wall and left.

Soon, we set off. Outside, there was some fuss. People were running around and shouting. Cars were being packed, ready to go. My inner voice was getting louder, telling me to make Maxim go right at that minute. But I did not say anything. I forced my emotions down inside me and waited.

When everybody was in the car, I started reading a prayer on my phone. Annya also joined me, repeating the words after me. We were afraid but ready to fight with any obstacles in our way. At that moment, we were decisive and as brave as we could be.

On the way, as it was nearby, Maxim suggested going to the garage to get some petrol before going home. So, we went there first.

While he was filling up, he looked at me. Seeing stress on my face, he asked, "What do you think? Do you want to go away now?"

"YESS! - I cried with relief, "I just think that we should go now without stopping."

"Okay, Let's go," he confirmed.

Suddenly, we heard a loud explosion near the garage. I was frightened but tried to calm the children. I screamed to Maxim, "Faster. We must go. Please, hurry up!"

Just at that moment, a man came up to him and asked for a funnel. He also needed to put petrol in his car. Maxim could not reject him, so he gave him his funnel and helped him with his car. We were waiting in our car and each second seemed like eternity.

For Maxim, helping a person was more important than saving himself. In spite of my fear inside, I agreed with his decision to help. I thought to myself that this deed held increased significance and weight because my husband was performing it while in severe danger. Even in the toughest of circumstances, in a moment where there was a risk of death, Maxim's selfless kindness could not be denied.

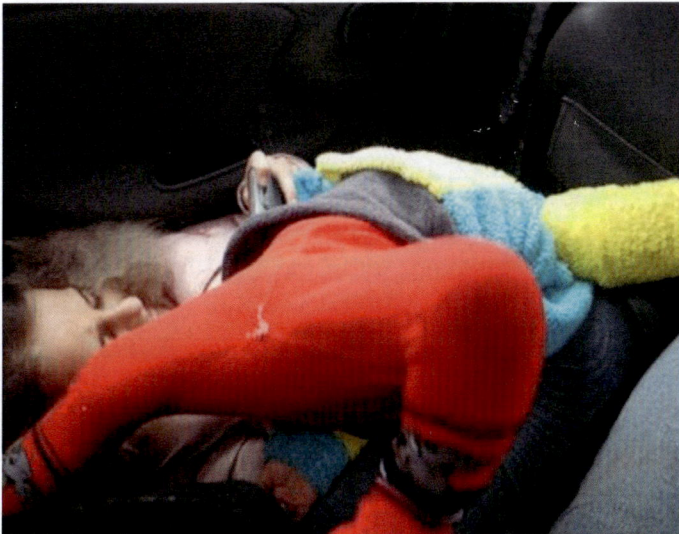

Somehow, in all the chaos, Annya and Lev get some sleep.

At last, we jumped into the car and went to the main road. Our main task for the day was to leave the city. Lev and Tishka were constantly crying which made our situation even more unbearable as well as dangerous. We should have been quiet on the road, but it was impossible. They did not understand what was going on and continued screaming as loud as they could. The intense situation was mixed with these cries, and every minute, we were at risk of being noticed by Russian soldiers.

The day before, I had read the news about one family from Kharkiv consisting of a mother, a father and three kids who were trying to escape. They had been shot by Russians on the motorway. Driving through the same place the next day, it was understandable that we would be terrified and we were.

It was as if we were on a road to hell. We were going past broken cars and destroyed houses. It was extremely hazardous and risky. Very soon, we were held up in a huge traffic jam, where we sat for more than five hours.

Thousands of cars were there, all trying to overtake and escape to safety. In our car, as well as all the crying, it was also, extremely cold and there was too little room for five people. The car heating system did not work, and even though we were all wearing warm clothes, we were trembling from the cold. Our car was very old and small, a gift from my grandfather before his death. Every bit of room was taken up with our possessions including Tishka. We held items on our knees, in our hands, and under our feet. We were packed into this tiny space like fish in a can.

Time dragged on endlessly, as if in slow motion. It was like a bad horror movie which would not end. Through the window, I could see how people were standing near their cars and waving to other drivers, asking for help. I could see women with little babies in their arms, walking on the motorway in the freezing cold. The situation was awful and unforgettably horrendous. It was a scene of despair and pain. I remember exactly what I saw, felt and wanted at that moment.

The most repetitive words in my soul were, 'God, save my children from the war, please, save their lives'. I did not want to leave my adorable city, Kharkiv, but I made the decision to protect my children. It was a sensible choice. It was the only choice. The lives and future of my children were obviously, more important than anything else for me.

Most of the way, I did not talk much with Maxim. We were going through turmoil inside but kept our pain hidden. I was sitting in the car and thinking about the war. 'What is our future? What can we do?' At that moment, the simple answer was NOTHING! Our life consisted only of little steps forwards but to where, we did not know.

Stuck in traffic for hours at a time.

I used the mantra, 'Step by step' all the time through this whole nightmare. It was all we could do.

However, it was very hard for me to accept this approach. All my life, I had been persistent and assertive. I always set my goals and especially when I experienced adversity, I clawed my way back into contention. I had never lived without pursuing big missions. I liked obstacles and used to repeat the phrase which was also written as a tattoo on my arm, 'No obstacles are ever insurmountable!'. But now, I was imprisoned by my circumstances. My future was dark. I just had to cling to whatever chances came my way and to survive. It was my only way to get through the hell.

We tried to find a place to stay at night in Poltava, a town just over ninety miles west of Kharkiv. It was almost dark. I dialled all the numbers which I found on the internet but almost all the places were engaged. We began to panic about what we could do. We were hungry, cold and exhausted. After twelve hours in the car with all the shooting and anxiety, we longed to stop somewhere for the night and have some sort of a break.

At last, we found a room in the college hostel in Poltava. We sighed with relief that we were heading somewhere. The first stage of our trial was almost resolved.

Finally, we arrived in Poltava at midnight, hungry, very tired and looking dishevelled. When we arrived at the hostel, a woman who we had spoken to on the phone, helped us to our room. Then, she took me to the warehouse and gave us a lot of clothes which we needed because we were dirty, and without anything to change into. We had driven away almost with nothing; all our possessions were at home. I was very grateful. I hugged the woman tightly. For her, it was nothing special, as she had a lot of bags with clothes from the citizens from Kharkiv. But for me, it was a real miracle. And her constant question: "Do you need anything else?" sounded like "I love you; you are in safety now. Be calm!"

It was very late; we collapsed with exhaustion. Unfortunately, we had eaten very little. We had run out of almost all our food and what we had left was terrible. I gulped the stew from the can and wanted to vomit. But we had to eat in spite of the disgusting taste and smell. We had no choice. 'Thank God for this food though', I thought.

Lev and Misha settle into our room in Poltava.

The most exciting moment for me was taking a shower. It was very cold inside the building and it took me several minutes to find it along the dark corridor. I took off my clothes and stepped in the freezing cabin. Even under such uncomfortable conditions, at once, I filled up with bliss and joy. The hot water felt exquisite. I was standing in the shower and almost crying from happiness. The shower room was not closed and everyone could come in. I was delighted with this marvellous combination of the water and the moment. The last time I had had a shower was before the day before war began, over two weeks before.

Then, at night, we put on all our warm clothes and went to bed. We were sleeping in jackets, coats and sweaters because it was extremely cold inside. When everybody fell asleep, I gazed at my children, my husband and the cat, curled up in my daughter's arms.

I was happy to see Tishka on the bed with Annya. This journey was extremely hard for him. He did not understand why he should be in the cage in the car for twelve hours and then live in a new, unfamiliar place. I saw how he tried to struggle with us. Without any protests, he went to the toilet and ate everything that we gave him. Tishka was in our team, a team of survivors. He was a member of our family and we all loved him so much.

Anyway, that night, I was speculating on the things to be happy about. We were in a real bed in a real room and safe at last. There were no bombs outside. It was silent. I liked the silence. Before, I had never realised the real meaning of silence, I had taken it for granted. But that night, I was praying and thankful for this safe night for all of us, for these kind people who gave us this shelter and for the food. Finally, with a smile on my face, I also fell asleep.

I had to wake up very early the next day, because I knew that the journey would be hard and there would be long queues again. Millions of Ukrainians were on the road heading westwards away from the fighting at the same time.

When I opened my eyes, I glanced at my kids in the beds and looked around the room. In the morning, it did not look as it had the night before. The walls were dirty, without wallpaper; there were no sheets on the beds; the furniture was old and broken.

This view took me back to the past, many years before, to when I had to move to the Donbass and had started my life from scratch. I met Maxim and we worked hard in order to buy our first flat in Kharkiv. We had been saving for years until we could afford to buy it, the flat of our dreams.

I remembered enjoying every aspect of it. I could not forget how much we had overcome before we were able to live in comfort; how long had we been living before in rented flats like this room. I reflected on my previous life in our last rented flat.

***

I was in bed with my man, Maxim who I loved so much and my son, Misha was sleeping in the armchair down at our feet. Suddenly, I woke up because Maxim kissed my shoulder. I turned around and kissed him back. That night without any words, we made our daughter, Annya. We did not have enough money for our future, and we did not know what we would do, but we loved each other and knew that we could do anything together. I became pregnant and our life changed dramatically. Money started coming from everywhere. Everybody helped. Our business was taking off, giving us bigger and bigger profits. Then, at last, we got our first flat in Kharkiv. Back then, we did not think about comfort. We focused on our happiness and love for each other. It united us and helped to cope with all our difficulties.

Now, the war showed us again that materialistic things were nothing compared with our love and unity. The best treasure in our life was our family, nothing else. We could live in the most drastic conditions but if we loved each other, nothing could prevent us from being happy.

***

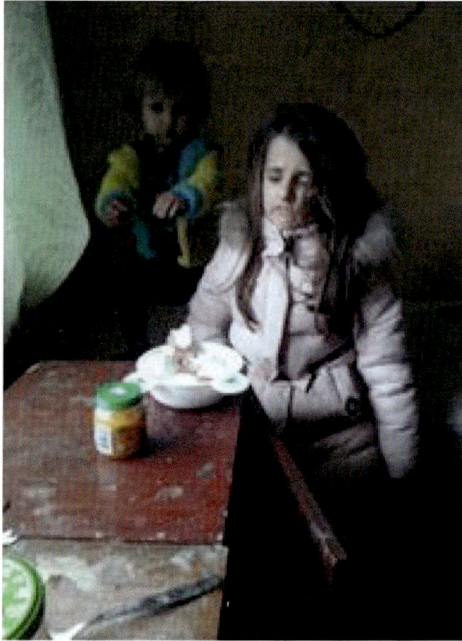

Lev and Annya have breakfast in Poltava.

Maxim called me and I had to pull myself away from my memories and come back to the present-day reality. I woke up the children and started packing the bags.

For breakfast, we cooked buckwheat with some pieces of disgusting and greasy meat from a can. I remembered how we ate it, stuffing the pieces in our mouths, wanting to vomit it back up. But we knew how important it was to eat before the long trip ahead. Even Lev tried to eat some food. We were preparing for a tough, new adventure.

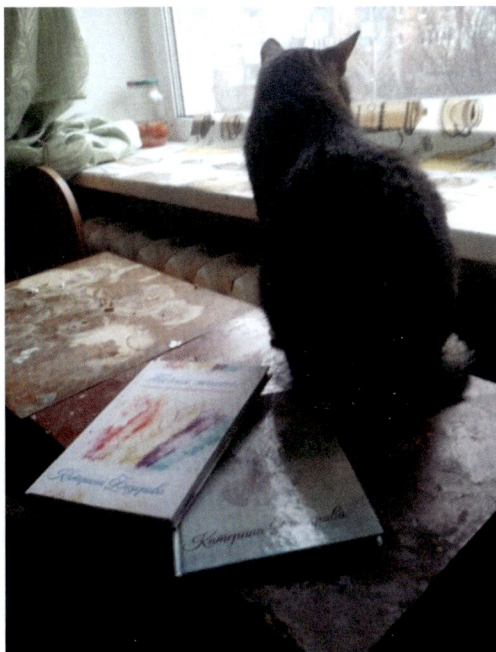

Tishka waits for our departure.

My family were already sitting in the car, and I ran back to find the woman who had helped us the day before by giving us shelter. I presented her with two of my own books. I wrote her some warm words and signed them, Thank you for everything that you did for my family. I will pray for you and will never forget your deed. Stay safe. I hope my books will inspire you and make you happy!'

"Don't mention it," she said. "It was a pleasure for me to help you. You're owed that. I am sure you will get a lot of help along your way. Now, it is time for you to get help from people." These words stayed in my head for a long time afterwards. They were so meaningful to me.

Soon, we were on our road again: a long and hellish road to nowhere.

Chapter 3

Open Doors and Open Hearts

Ask for help. Receiving is an act of generosity
— Cheryl Richardson

When we left the hostel, we anticipated more difficulties and traffic jams on the road but we were ready for anything. We were moving from one city to another, step by step going further and further west, away from death and war.

After Poltava, our new destination was going to be Kropyvnytskyi, a town over one hundred and fifty miles away by car. As a destination, this city emerged for us by chance. On Facebook, a woman called Olga, who liked my posts and had bought my books, offered us a helping hand. When Kharkiv was bombed severely, she sent me a private message saying that we could go to her and stay in her house for as long as we wanted. Even though we did not know her at all, we accepted her proposal and headed for our new home. In all honesty, we had no idea where we would end up.

We just kept going and going, listening to our soul and interpreting the signs along the way. Sometimes, I felt that I was followed by God and that I should just accept what was being offered by people and situations. I trusted everything that was going on in my life. I turned off my fear and accepted what was happening. We moved on.

On the way, we stopped to buy some food. I went into the shop and saw many products on the shelves: sausages, bread and other delicious things. While I was standing in a queue, suddenly, I burst into tears. I sobbed. I realised that we could eat real food. Also, this possibility was so near to me, right there in front of me. I saw the shop assistant who was smiling as she handed out people's shopping to them. While I was crying, I noticed another woman on the other side of the shop. She was also in tears looking at the bread. We caught each other's eye and understood each other at that moment. We did not say anything but felt each other's emotions.

The war had taught us to value most things. Before the conflict, we had thrown away a lot of food, not understanding or appreciating that somebody else was dying from hunger at that moment somewhere else. But now, after our own experience of surviving on minimum amounts of food, we were looking at a loaf of bread and crying. A simple loaf had taken on a new significance in our lives.

I came back to our car with a big bag full of food. The smell from the sausage I had bought was very strong and my kids begged me to give them some. I allowed them to take a few pieces but not too many because we could not be sure when we would be able to get more. The war was teaching us to think about the next day as well as the next hour.

Time on the road was certainly very challenging. We sat in queues for ages, sometimes not moving for three or four hours at a stretch. At the same time, my friend, Yana, was driving with her family on the same road, so we called each other to give each other support. We were like birds flying to warm places from pain and danger, seeking safety and maybe, a paradise.

It was getting dark, as we approached Kropyvnytskyi. But suddenly, we were stopped by Ukrainian soldiers at a roadblock and asked to change our route, because it was dangerous on the itinerary we were on. We had no choice and went in the direction they suggested. At night, in the dark, we tried to find Olga's address for hours.

The children were hungry and exhausted. Lev and Tishka were crying non-stop and it was extremely cold in the car. We wanted to find a resting place where we could stop at last, and sleep.

Soon, our wishes were granted. Finally, we arrived at Olga's house. She was waiting for us with her two children. She had not slept and was worried about us; she had been calling and writing all the way. At eleven o'clock at night, we arrived, took off our coats and of course, let our tormented cat out of the cage. Tishka examined the territory, and immediately, made new friends, Olga's two cats. He was also tired and hungry, but happy to be free at last.

Olga's house looked so sweet and cosy. She laid the table with Ukrainian borsch and spaghetti with cutlets. It tasted unbelievably delicious. We ate greedily, from time to time, looking around us mechanically checking the environment. Olga gave us not just food, she presented a blissful moment of happiness for us. We were severely tired but now, we were so happy. We were able to enjoy the taste of superb tasting food. This late supper was the brightest and the most wonderful moment we had experienced since the beginning of the war.

Before bed, we went to have a bath. It was like another gift from God. I cannot forget the moment I lay in the water and relaxed. I was overwhelmed with emotions. I experienced a fresh injection of hope for a better future.

I closed my eyes as I lay in the warmth and again, dived back into my past life.

***

I returned to when my Lev was born. His birth gave me the chance to change my life and a lot of things did change. I was transformed significantly. I started writing extensively. Hundreds of poems and stories were born in a short period of time. I could not understand what was going on. I was inspired so much that I wrote and wrote. I sat for hours at night in front of the screen and printed out what I had typed almost non-stop. I was an English teacher who had suddenly become an obsessive writer. I could not imagine life without books.

My three books were published in just two years. How come? For me, it seemed incredible. I revealed my inner gift to the world. All my books were bought all over Ukraine. I was excited to perform on stages sharing wise words and advice from my texts. This period of my life was the brightest. I had taken the books from my last publication with us from our flat in Kharkiv but for what? I was here in Kropyvnytskyi and going nowhere. These books reminded me about how happy I had been and what success I had managed to achieve for a short period.

I reflected on these light sparkles in my past lying in the bath and feeling a wave of satisfaction in my relaxing body.

I was over the moon.

***

After my bath, I went to bed, hugged Lev tightly and kissed Maxim. This night was much better and more comfortable than the previous one. As usual, I thanked God for everything and for everyone on that day and fell asleep quickly. My family and I were alive, a true reason for happiness.

The morning started at seven when Lev woke up screaming loudly. It seemed as if he was reminding us about the continuation of our journey. We got up and went lazily to the kitchen. Olga had prepared delicious pancakes and hot mugs with coffee and tea were waiting for us. We had to go but we were not ready for the next trial, just yet. We had not recharged our batteries. We were not full of energy at all. Also, we still did not know where to go next.

Having weighed all the pros and cons, we decided to stay longer in Olga's house. We allowed ourselves to have a break and stop for a while. We also had to think about our next stop and where exactly would be our final destination. We could not know for sure if we would manage to cross the border with Romania all together. On the one hand, we had three children, and it was permitted to let families with men and three children across, but on the other hand, it was possible that we did not have enough documents for our elder son Misha, because he was born in my first marriage. That's why it was a risk to go through the border with Maxim. He could have been taken into the military. We were not ready to split up. Via social media, we wrote to hundreds of acquaintances to ask for advice. Where should we move to? Obviously, I asked this question to my soul millions of times seeking any inner signs. Nothing was clear in my heart. My fear of losing Maxim and my courage to go to the best place for my family were churning inside me. I could not decide what was right.

Meanwhile, in Kharkiv, there were more and more dangerous battles. I looked at the photos of a broken building in my district where we had been recently, standing in a queue in the shop. There had been a huge explosion exactly on the place where Maxim had been standing several days before trying to buy medicine for me. He might have been killed at that moment. My heart trembled.

In the evening, my mum called me. She was crying and talking about her worries for me.

"My beloved daughter, it is so sad. I've just found you and this war can now take you from me. I am so afraid of losing you again," she said.

"Mum, don't cry. At the moment, I am okay. I hope we will find a safer place and can stop at last," I tried to reassure her.

"How do you feel?" she asked.

"I am still ill. Perhaps, I need to take some medicine. I will go to the chemist now and find something," I replied.

"Yes. Don't forget about yourself. You must be strong for your family. They depend on you," she said and started crying again.

"What happened, mum?" I asked her.

"I've thought about your grandmother. She died before the war and we are still mourning. But, on the other hand, she can't see everything that is going on now. She doesn't see how much you are suffering and going through. Maybe, God wanted to protect her from this pain and took her earlier?" she suggested.

"Yes, you are right. We should trust his decisions. I needed her so much, but I accepted her leaving," I confirmed.

"Tell me about everything that you and your family have had to overcome. I want to know everything about you now," she insisted to know.

I told her about our journey and all our trials. She listened carefully and expressed her support and empathy.

After her call, I went for a short walk to the chemist. As I walked along the streets, I thought about the conversation with my mother. We had an uncertain relationship with each other.

***

When I was four, my mother gave me to my grandmother. Without explaining anything, she took me to her house with my things and closed the door. I haven't forgotten that day until now. I remembered every detail.

There was an almost empty bedroom, a slightly subdued light and strange unclear conversation between the two women. I could not understand the reason why she did it or if she would come back again. I felt lonely and lost. When she went away, I stayed with Grandmother Elena. My young heart was broken. I might have made the decision to remember this betrayal and delete all the memories with my mother forever. She left me and she took my love with her. But something prevented me from doing that.

The years went by. My grandmother invested in me very much. I had private teachers, wore the trendiest clothes, and had everything that I asked for. But I always needed and wanted my mother's care. I strongly believed that in order to get her attention, I should be a very successful girl, diligent and kind. I could not take love for granted, I always tried to prove that I deserved to be loved. I struggled all the time for a little piece of people's care. I was afraid that if I did not do that, in the end, they would leave me like my mother had done once. So, I strived every time to be a better version of myself. I was a model pupil at school and finished it with a silver medal. I participated in all varieties of competitions and always won. I wanted my mother to be proud of me. Later, I graduated from university with a law degree and got A's for all subjects. I did not like my law education. It was my grandmother who pressured me to study there. I was against it but powerless to stop my grandmother's influence. She was a bossy woman who never accepted any opinions different from hers.

All my life, I found myself proving to everyone that I was not a bad person. There was really heavy baggage on my soul. This psychological trauma affected me almost all the way through my years growing up. Unfortunately, I could not change how I was programmed.

On the eve before the war, in autumn, my grandmother died. She was ill with Coronavirus and stayed in Makeevka, which was occupied by Russia. So, I could not go to her to help or to buy her medicine. In the hospital, in much agony, she died.

I remembered my mother's call and her words, "Your grandmother died. Sorry ..."

I threw the phone on the floor and cried so loud. No, it wasn't crying; it was an animal wailing. Lev and my daughter, Annya were at home. I could not stop crying. I beat my head on the floor as if I wanted to give myself more pain. Annya became quite concerned about me, even a bit scared and came to ask me if I was okay.

My grandmother's death destroyed me so much. It took me several months to get back to normal. My mother called me every day and we prayed for granny. It brought us together. Once I had a nightmare about my grandmother. She asked me to forgive her and to restart the relationship with my mother. She explained that she would not come to me in dreams anymore and asked me to stop asking for her. That made me angry at her. It seemed to me like betrayal again. But I promised to try and from that day, my mother and I called each other often. But soon, the war stopped our idyllic chatting.

***

My thoughts were interrupted by a siren in the city. People were rushing to leave the streets. I hastily crossed the road and came to the chemist. I needed some medicine and antibiotics for my sore throat. I looked around and the shelves were almost empty. I bought the last of the antibiotics, some pills and cough mixture. Then, I rushed back to Olga's house.

We were running away from the war but the war was chasing us. I felt we needed to go further away and not stay where we were for longer as the war would catch us up. We needed to find a safer place. We had to cross the border and go to another European country to ask for shelter. It was necessary for our children. The closer I got to the house, the more I wanted to talk about my decision to take a risk to go to the border. If we did not try, we would always wonder if we had missed an opportunity. I estimated that we had about a fifty-fifty chance of success. Despite the risk of failure, it was an opportunity. If we could get out of the country, we would be able to save our family.

I was so eager to share my thoughts. I could not wait. I stepped into the house.

"Maxim, we must leave the country. We can do it," I said.

"But it is such a risk," he replied. "I might be taken to the army and you will have to travel alone." But I saw in his eyes a sign of hope. He might have been thinking about it too.

"I have a plan," I said confidently and looked at him filled with excitement and determination. The plan had come to me suddenly.

"I can write to my friend, who helps Ukrainians. He has offered me his help. I will call him and ask for advice. Believe me and my intuition. It saved our lives recently," I assured him.

"You are right. Carry on with your plan. I am hesitating but ready to follow whatever you suggest," he confirmed.

I took my mobile phone and went to the bedroom to call my friend, Eduard. He was happy to explain to me how to cross the border. He assured me that we had a good chance and that we should go to the Romanian border. He proposed that we stay in the hotel where he was located at that time. He promised to book a room for us. I was filled with positive thoughts after the conversation with him. Later, I shared everything with Maxim.

"Okay," he agreed, "I am ready to try. It is risky but it is worth doing." We were agreed that after a couple of days staying with Olga, we would move on.

Through the second part of the day, we were all in a good mood chatting together, drinking tea and anticipating the success of our next move. We wanted to hope for the best. We were so tired of moving from place to place in search of food and shelter.

In the evening, I talked to Olga and we realised that it wasn' t an accident that we had met; that the war had given us a gift in joining together our destinies. Since that day, we have been best friends. Before our meeting, I had never known a person like her, who could understand and accept me, my soul and my inner world so well.

We chatted for several hours and could not stop, finding many things to talk about that we had in common. We were like sisters. I also presented her with my books and I took photographs of her. She liked how she looked in the photos which I had taken of her. Actually, Olga was an incredibly attractive woman: dark sparkling hair and deep, green eyes. She reminded me of a gracious queen. Her beauty was so exquisite and unique.

The lovely Olga. In Kropyvnytskyi,
she gave us her home to stay in.

Later, we spoke a lot about beauty and how it is important to accept yourself and your appearance. I wanted to share my thoughts with her.

"God gives us our body for certain reasons. It cannot be ugly or inappropriate. It is a gift for us. We should take it as an inseparable part of us and our lives. If we hadn't had a slightly different appearance, we would have had another life scenario: other people, other hobbies, jobs, etc. We are always beautiful. There is not any beauty standard for God, because we are always perfect."

I told Olga about my way of accepting my beauty. For many years, I had a lot of complexes because of my nose, my thin body and other drawbacks which I had been made aware of often. It seemed to me the whole world was gossiping just about me and my ugliness. I did not believe anyone who persistently reassured me that I was beautiful. I had dates with so many boys and they complimented me trying to inspire me and increase my confidence but I was deaf to their words. I was confident that God had not given me beauty and I was an ugly duckling. In my family, everyone's comments seemed to confirm what I believed. Everyone often talked about my ugly nose and my thinness. Even my mother agreed with me that one day, I should have surgery on my nose.

It took me many years of trials and betrayals to realise at last, that my view of myself was false. Step by step, I started to notice how my face and body were necessary for everything in my life. And I started to love them. I looked at the mirror and saw a charming girl who came to this world in this body to change things for others for the better. I came to the conclusion: the more you love yourself, the more you will love other people and the more other people will love you. It is a vital triangle of love which all people must know. I came to this realisation at the age of thirty-three.

Olga hugged me after this honest and intimate conversation. We went to her room. She gave me so many things of hers. My luggage was becoming heavier and heavier after each stop we made. The women from Poltava and now Olga, had not only given me a stay for a night; they had helped to build me up. In a way, they were making me whole. I felt I was turning into a real person again. I was like a broken structure, which was now reconstructed again.

Furthermore, she proposed that I could leave my books in her house and she would try to sell them. If she did, she would send me the money. It sounded unbelievable but I agreed. There was no space in the car anymore anyway. I did not want to throw them out. I also left her a book called *Gift* by Edith Eger. My wise daughter Annya had taken two books for me from our flat: this one and *The Tattooist of Auschwitz*.

"Annya, why these books?" I had asked her with amazement.

"They are real for you now. They are about the war too. I suppose they will be useful," she said.

Lev enjoys the bath.
It was just like being back at home.

These books were important for me and I wanted to take them but I decided to give Olga something that was valuable for me. After all, if we present something that is very significant for us, we express the biggest love to the person we are presenting the gift to, a present from our heart. Olga was such an important person and I wanted to share my treasure with her.

Before bed, all my children took a bath. They were so happy and excited playing in the water.

"Mum! Mum," they kept calling. For those few moments, I felt like I was back at home. It reminded me of the happy days in our flat in Kharkiv.

That night, I went to bed with hope and a smile. Actually, it was my first night with such a feeling. I was so grateful for everyone and everything that day. I looked around the room where we were lying and thought that we were so lucky to meet such lovely and kind people on the way. God protected us and took us forward.

Chapter 4

Endless Traffic and Helping Hands

I am grateful for all the trials
that made me a better person
— Lailah Gifty Akita

There was a new day and again, a new road to take us further to the west. It was very early in the morning when we took our places in the car and began our journey to the next stop in our itinerary. Our next stay was scheduled to be in Uman, a drive of just over one hundred miles.

Again, there were long queues on the roads, traffic jams which lasted for many hours. But we were lucky to arrive in Uman comparatively early. It was about five o'clock in the evening.

However, we had to face a serious problem: where to stay for a night. Unfortunately, we did not have anybody in this city who could help us with even just one little room. The city was overfilled with refugees. Soon, the curfew in the city was about to start. This meant nobody should stay outside. It was forbidden to leave safe places at this time.

First, I searched for shelter on the internet, but I did not come up with anything. Most of the listed numbers were out of service and the places I did manage to make contact with were full. Then, Maxim ran around the city centre knocking at different doors while we were waiting in the car. We were ready to pay any money to have dinner and some rest. Lev was crying and wanted to get out of the car, but I kept the doors locked. I prayed and waited for Maxim. Our car was in the city centre and we could see how many people were moving around the square with heavy bags and frightened eyes. They were also lost in an unfamiliar city, hoping for better.

At last, I saw a silhouette of my husband in the distance. I was anticipating the news he was about to share with us. Could we stay somewhere for the night or would we have to sleep in the car?

At last, he came to us shaking hands excitedly.

"We did it!" he shouted through the car window, "It was the last room in the hotel."

"Really?" I said, amazed and relieved.

"Yes, something from the sky is really helping us." Suddenly, a room appeared for us from nowhere. So, we paid for it straight away. Believe me, it was a real jackpot. Tired but happy, we approached the hotel with dozens of bags, a crying cat in the cage and a sleeping Lev.

The hotel was in the heart of the city. In the hall, there were so many people shouting and asking for rooms. We had the keys, as Maxim had already paid money for a night, so we went straight to our room. I carried Lev while holding Annya's hand. We were anticipating a warm place with a bed and shower and kept going upstairs. I looked back at the hundreds of people in the hall. They were in despair, extremely exhausted and hungry. I felt sorry for them, I understood them well; we had overcome the same situation.

When we entered the room, we jumped on the bed all together. We had been sitting in the car for so long, and our legs and back were really painful. We just wanted to feel relief and get some rest.

The hotel room was tiny for five of us. There was just one bed and two pillows. I went downstairs to ask for a bed for the little child and some extra sheets for the bed and extra pillows. The receptionist helped with everything. They found a cot for a baby and gave us some bed sets. Annya decided to sleep in the cot, and the rest of us slept on the bed.

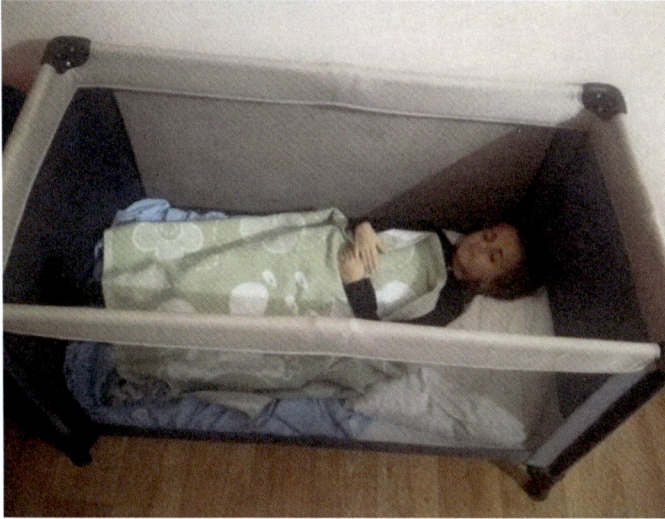

Annya opts for the cot to sleep in.
How peaceful she looks despite all the disruption.

The children fell asleep very quickly but Maxim and I could not sleep; we were thinking about the risk of crossing the border.

I went to take a shower, as I wanted to fill myself with energy and positivity. Water always helps me. I was standing under the water catching the drops with my mouth. At that moment, I thought about Maxim, how strongly I loved him and, maybe, I could see him, talk to him, touch him in the last days. We were not sure that our operation on the border would be successful. I started crying. He knocked at the shower booth, wanting to join me in the shower. I let him in. We did not say a word but started kissing each other. This moment might be our last intimate moment together. We touched each other so softly, as if it was our first time. I felt his love through his stroking, touching, kissing. It was very sincere and heartfelt. We were loving each other so passionately, it was more than just simple physical contact, it was as if our souls were uniting. Maybe, we might never make love to each other again but our love for each other would last forever.

After such soulful affinity, we fell asleep together, lying in the centre of the bed with one son on either side of each of us. We accepted the chance that the night could be our last experience of closeness and we were just happy to enjoy every minute being together.

Next morning, we had a plan to reach Ternopil. This was a town a bit further away. It was just under two hundred and fifty miles from where we were by road. I wrote a message on Facebook to ask for help with accommodation for or a night. One girl wrote to me in messenger. Then, she asked another friend to help us. A new friend, another Olga, had offered to give us a helping hand. She invited us to her flat where she was living with her parents. She did not know anything about us, just that I was an English teacher and that I was with my husband and three children going to the border.

Without hesitating, we headed straight for Ternopil, not worried about the night ahead. We were going to stay in Olga's flat.

The road was again hard. There were a lot of cars, standing for hours, going nowhere. While we were going through Vinnitsa, suddenly we heard a huge explosion. The city airport was severely bombed. A lot of fire engines headed to the destroyed airport. The war siren was ringing everywhere. The sky was mixed with clouds and smoke. We understood that we were stuck in the city and could not go further anymore today.

Stationary in another traffic jam.
Lev tries to take the wheel.

Also, we had very little petrol left and all the petrol stations were almost empty. Some working ones were surrounded by many cars. We had no choice; we had to wait in one of the endless queues. The line of cars went for several kilometres. When the siren was working, all the shops were closed. The kids were hungry but we did not know how long we were going to wait for petrol. It did not look like there was any possibility of getting to Ternopil that day.

I felt lost, but I tried to calm down and soothe everybody in the car. We had to come up with a new plan and make new decisions.

"I think we should find a room in this city. I will try to find one on the internet," I said to Maxim.

"Yes, I feel the same," he answered desperately.

"Maybe, there will be some hotels again. I have never been to this city before. I know nothing here," I continued as I began to search.

"Me too." He said, "But we will have to be stuck here. It is obvious, unfortunately."

While we were waiting in the queue, I tried to surf the internet, Facebook and other websites to find something.

Luckily, I was given a number of a religious organisation which helped refugees. I called them and they gave us an address where we could go. It was a miracle. Again, we had received a helping hand.

I watch over Annya and Lev in the car.

Plus, it was not so far from the place where we were. We sighed with relief, called Olga in Ternopil and explained the situation, informing her that we would come to her the next day.

After two hours of standing in a queue for petrol, at last we filled up our car. Then, we drove to the address we had been given in Vinnitsa. Our arrival in Ternopil would have to wait.

A lovely woman met us with a smile and hugs. They were religious people, so for them, it was very important to help people in the war. They helped everyone who was moving through their city. God again helped us by sending such open and generous people. She took us to a very comfortable house. There were two cosy rooms, a lovely bathroom and a kitchen. Her mother gave us a big saucepan with hot soup, which seemed divinely delicious after the hard drive.

I was so excited and grateful. Everything happened so quickly that we hardly believed it. It was like a fairy-tale.

Nevertheless, the situation in the city was not calm. We could see a big cloud above the airport in the distance and heard the sirens from time to time. As we moved, the war moved too, chasing us step by step.

After we ate soup and had a rest for a while, I went to the shop nearby. It was such a beautiful place. I was going along the streets and enjoying picturesque views, historical buildings, old churches and very neatly built detached houses. For me, it was like a magic place. I fell in love with the city.

Everyone I met was friendly, helping me to find a shop and talking about everything while carefully avoiding the topic of the war. My voice was still hoarse, but I could speak with them in Ukrainian. I was happy that I could speak my country's language better and better. People were waiting politely until I remembered some Ukrainian words.

Having bought all the necessary groceries, I rushed home to make my kids happy with everything that I had bought for them. Going to the shops now was not something which we took for granted. It was a lucky opportunity and gave us excitement and happiness. We rejoiced every time when we could buy something. We were like hunters fighting for food and other necessities.

In the evening, the owner of the house, came to us and we had a friendly conversation. She told us about her mission to help people. I told her that she helped us so much and that I was not used to receiving so much help.

She answered, "Blessed is one who receives help, not just the one who gives it. You should be able to get help from people. Maybe, all this adventure is necessary for you to learn this lesson."

"Maybe ... " I answered thoughtfully, "But you know, I have helped people during all my life. I have been a volunteer since I was sixteen. I worked with people struggling with cancer, disabled people and orphans. I was happy to do it, because it gave me a sense of life, and it inspired me so much. And now, a lot of people are helping me. It is so unusual for me."

"Yes, but it is normal. You should allow people to realise their goodness. It is also important for them, the same as for you. Now, you can open your heart and accept all kind deeds from everyone else," she continued.

"Your words are very wise. I must think about them," I replied.

Her words got stuck in my mind for a long time. I knew about the necessity of doing good things to people, but I had never thought about taking help back. How important it is to be able to receive God's help. And this woman had reiterated the phrase which I heard from the other woman in the hostel in Poltava, then Olga in Kropyvnytskyi. I was sure that these words were vital food for me.

Tishka in his cage. This time, on the front seat.

Around us, there are so many opportunities, which might have been given by God. He can help us through other people, by their hands. Sometimes, we miss those chances, avoid this help, thinking that we are not worth it or we are too arrogant. But in such a way, we do not get what we actually ask from God. It is our failure, our misfortune. And besides it, we do not give another person an opportunity to realise their mission. So, this woman was right about my ignorance of other people's help. Their help for me was as vital as my help for them.

All through our journey, my new friend Olga from Kropyvnytskyi and my aunt Toma both called me and wrote to me. They were worried about me and my family. Thanks to their support, my steps were not so painful and unbearable. I knew that there was somebody who was thinking about us and it gave me power to go further and further.

My aunt Toma was a very close person to me. She helped my grandmother to bring me up. She played a significant role in my life and did a lot for me. She was also living under Russian occupation and we had no chance to see each other. We could just phone and dreamed about the end of the war and a long-awaited meeting.

We went to bed early, because the next day we wanted to get up again at dawn to make a start for our new target, Ternopil. Olga and her family were waiting for us there.

Luckily, we were full of energy after sleeping and eating enough, so we were ready to take on the challenges of the next stage of our trip and get to Ternopil quickly. We were decisive and determined. After so many trials, we were turning into battle-hardened people.

We drove fast and fortunately, the road was not blocked with a lot of traffic jams. When my kids were sleeping, I was thinking again about crossing the border and the possible risks for Maxim. Thousands of questions were prowling through my mind. There was no escaping the constant negative voices. My head was against this plan, but something was whispering inside of my heart, "Go. You can do it!" At such moments, I was filled with hope and was looking forward to being on the other side of the border as soon as possible.

We arrived in Ternopil at three o'clock in the afternoon. It was the earliest arrival we had made. We easily found Olga's house. She and her parents greeted us with open hugs. They were such kind and lovely people. They gave us a lunch of delicious borsh and lovely items from the bakery.

We let Tishka out of the cage and he was happy to feel free around their flat. There were also two cats, who did not want to have a competitor on their territory. So, there were fights from time to time. Tishka was younger and weaker after his road trip, so they usually beat him and stole his food.

My voice became a bit better so I accepted a proposal to perform for the Jewish National Television Channel and describe the situation about the war and our difficult trip. I wrote to the woman from this channel and arranged to be online at nine o'clock in the evening. Of course, I was totally afraid because it was live news and I could not speak well yet. I was still ill and weak. But my fear and hesitation were not stronger than my desire to do something for my country, to tell the truth and ask people from Israel to help Ukraine. I was looking forward to the broadcast.

During the day, I went to the shop to buy some medicine and groceries, played with the kids and chatted with Olga and her mother and father. In the evening, I started writing a speech for the Israeli people. I would need to speak in English, so I had to prepare my words in advance.

This is what I said.

'I am in Ternopil with my three children and my husband. We had to move from one city to another, trying to find safety. The war started on 24 February. This day changed my life dramatically. Before the war, I had everything: my lovely flat, cottage house, my own business. I considered myself to be a successful person. But that day, bombs started to drop on my city, on my country. We were sitting on the floor, trembling and asking God to save us. My seven-year-old daughter was crying heavily, reading a prayer many times over and over again.

'Taking into account the dangerous situation, we decided to move to a safer place and stayed in our school. We waited for a miracle, hoping that all this hell would finish and the Russians would realize their mistake and would go back home. But the situation became worse and worse. Bombs were falling more and more often. Russian tanks were moving on the motorway from Belgorod. We were sitting on the floor near the walls and listening to the approaching sounds of planes and bombs. This pressure made us crazy, I was worried about my family. After two weeks, we decided to take a risk and leave the city. And every day for twelve hours with three children and a cat we moved from one city to another. Now we are here. These kind people gave us shelter for a night, but tomorrow we will go again. I do not know when this endless, survival race will finish. We do not know where we should go nor where we can feel safe. This war destroyed my dreams and my husband's life and the future of our kids. Our parents have not been able to keep in touch with us since the beginning of the war. They might be dead now ...

'My country is being obliterated by Russia and the world is afraid to help us ... Please, help my country, give us a helping hand. It is not fair!'

When I wrote the last line, I burst into tears. It was so painful to go over everything again. I relived it in my memory again and I was going to live through it again when I spoke the words on camera. Again pain, again struggle ...

Later, we had a tasty meal in the kitchen, chatting about everything. But my thoughts were far from this. I was thinking ahead to my interview on the Jewish channel.

My broadcasting moment was approaching. I looked awful. I was sitting in the kitchen and waiting for the command to start speaking. My hair had become almost white since the start of the war because of stress and fear. I was wearing old and baggy clothes, which were given to me in Poltava. And I looked exhausted and thin as I had lost five kilograms during all our trials due to stress and a lack of food.

I was extremely nervous and my hoarse voice meant that I could not speak properly. But in two minutes, I would be speaking to the world.

The girl from the channel told me to be prepared. We checked the camera and sound.

I started saying my text which I had learned by heart. I was determined to do my best.

It was my war, where I was trying to overcome my fear in order to give a little help for my country. This help looked insignificant; it was just a drop in the ocean. My duty was to make as many such drops as I could.

When I spoke, towards the end of my words, a presenter interrupted me at the moment when I was asking for help. Maybe, it was deliberate, or maybe, the time was over. But I said the last phrase as loud as I could with my hoarse voice, "HELP US, PLEASE!"

When the broadcasting was over, I sighed with relief and fell back in my chair.

"I did it," I yelled loudly. "I really did it!"

When I came out of the kitchen, everybody was in their beds. Misha and Annya were sleeping together on one narrow bed in the same room where Olga was sleeping. Lev and Tishka were waiting for me.

I looked at them with love.

"I love you, my little kittens," I whispered softly.

They hugged me from both sides and fell asleep. I could not get to sleep quickly after this nervous event. It had been a real challenge for me. My words were going around and around in my head; my emotions were overwhelming. Then suddenly, worries about Maxim added to my mind. Tomorrow was going to be day 'X' when we would attempt to cross the border into Romania. Everything would be decided. I was lying in the bed, thinking about a possible bad scenario and crying. I did not want our family to be destroyed. We were like a big universe. Each of us was part of a very important system. Without even one part, our system could not work. We depended on each other. We were strong if only we were together. So, I believed that we would be able to overcome this obstacle and cross the border together, hand-in-hand.

Furthermore, Maxim had a birthday the next day. I had bought a chocolate cake and one big candle for him in the city centre during the afternoon. It was a surprise for him and my kids. In spite of the war and a risk of being split up, I was planning to celebrate his birthday with him and the children.

I was falling asleep and my tears were drying up on my cheeks. I kept repeating the same phrase, whispering, "I believe in better … I believe in better …"

Chapter 5

Risky Venture and a New Foreign Life

To avoid trials is to avoid living;
the more you go through, the more you learn
— Matshona Dhliwayo

In the morning, we woke up and quickly gathered all our things. We were ready for our big trial. We were going to cross the border with Romania. Olga helped us to pack everything in the car and wished us good luck.

We started our journey; there was no traffic jam. The weather was fine. We wanted to think positively. Nothing boded ill for our trip.

When we were already on our way, Olga called to inform us that I had forgotten my bag with my photo camera and all the equipment for it, my women's possessions and other memorable things which were very important to me. Of course, the most expensive of all the things was my camera, which was my working tool. I was supposed to earn money as a photographer. We did not know what to do, because we had already driven too far to turn back. It was sad to tell her to leave my camera in her flat, for a while at least.

This news was a big let-down, but it was a drop in the ocean compared to a bigger obstacle, that of crossing the border. I managed to let the thoughts about my camera go away and I turned my mind to this upcoming challenge.

We reached the Romanian border checkpoint very quickly and stopped. There was a queue of cars for several kilometres. We would have to stay in it for hours. It seemed endless, stretching out into the distance.

We moved forward very slowly. The atmosphere in the car was stressful. I was reading prayers non-stop. It seemed as if I might have read one prayer more than a thousand times. Lev was crying all the time. The children were begging us to eat. They were tired as well as hungry. I tried to help with everything. But my thoughts were about one task: crossing the border as soon as possible. I looked through the window and saw loads of men saying goodbye to their wives and children. Someone was sitting in the driver's seat and it meant that these men were going to cross the border. I was frightened and trembling, sitting in our car contemplating the oncoming situation. In some ways, at that moment, I was much more agitated than the time when we were sitting under the bombs in our school. I could not imagine my life without Maxim, especially now, during the war. I felt helpless.

At last, we arrived at customs. A customs officer came to our car and took our documents.

"So, the process has already started. I hope everything will be fine," Maxim said, trying to calm me down.

"Okay. I feel like we can do it. But ..." I started to reply.

Then suddenly, the officer came back and said strictly, "Open the windows."

He was a man about fifty, with a harsh voice and strict face. He looked very angry.

"Why does your son have another surname?" he demanded to know in a louder voice.

"He is my son from my first marriage," I answered and waited for his reaction.

"No way. Drive to the right side. You will have big problems!" he concluded.

My heart was aching, and my hands were trembling severely; I had an ache in my stomach. Many questions were swimming in my head. What can we do? Is it the end of our journey? Maxim will be taken to the army and I will stay here with three children and a cat in the cage. I cannot drive. Can we go further or do we have to stay in Ukraine? Maybe, we will find a room in the western part of Ukraine and I will be near my husband. Simultaneously, I was planning my life without Maxim, trying to imagine how we would survive without our possessions and on foot, and also thinking desperately about what we could do to change the situation.

Maxim was confused. He was standing near the car and waiting for the customs officer's decision. I was not ready to give up so quickly. We had documents which confirmed that we had three children. We had passports of a multi-child family and due to the law, we had a legal right to cross the border together. 'I must try!' I screamed in my soul.

I went to the customs room. I was holding Lev. He was crying and he was without boots, as I was so lost at that moment and did not notice that they had fallen off somewhere.

"Hello. Who can I speak to about our situation?" I asked loudly.

A young man appeared next to me.

"What has happened?" he asked calmly.

"We were stopped because my older son has another surname. Yes, it is a fact, but ... " I began to answer.

"Stop," he said. "Let's start from the beginning. Give me your documents first."

I gave him everything that we had. He asked more and more questions and I provided more and more papers. Unfortunately, we did not have a document from my ex-husband in which he refused to accept his son. He was in Moscow. All he had said when the war started was, "Sorry, but Putin did the necessary thing. He did not have any other choice. Ukraine behaved badly and must be punished." Since then, we had not kept in touch. I was not resentful of him, but

I could not communicate with the person who wanted both my death and that of his son.

I was trying to prove to the customs officer that Maxim had three children and he had been bringing them up for many years. He had been living with us since Misha was four years old. We also managed to find some extra documents from the scans on my telephone. I was struggling like a lion. I remember being so determined and firm. Every time, I found an answer when the officer stated a new sentence with the word "but ..." Maxim stood and watched our fight. In the end, the young man said, "Okay, you can go. Everything is okay."

"Thank you," I answered. I cannot describe the relief I felt at that moment. My behaviour switched quickly from a fighting girl to a kind one.

"Sorry, what is your name?" I asked the officer with a smile.

"Why do you need it?" he demanded to know.

"I want to pray for you," I replied.

He did not say his name. But God knows it, so I have been praying for this young officer ever since. I was very grateful to him. We did not do anything criminal, everything was done correctly, but the human factor can play a crucial role in such situations and I think it did in our case.

I returned straight to the car with Lev while Maxim went to complete all the documentation. In ten minutes, we resumed our journey again.

In the car, we sat silently. We did not believe that we had managed to go through this hell. Soon, we would be in Romania where we would struggle with new obstacles, but that would be later ... Tears flowed down my cheeks. I hugged Lev and cuddled Annya.

Suddenly, Misha broke our silence.

"Mum, I do not understand. Were you able to solve the problems relating to me? Is dad okay? Sorry that you have problems because of me ..." Misha said guiltily.

He seemed to be worried about us, about Maxim and thought that it was his fault.

"Misha, you are not a problem. You are a part of our team; we are a family. I do not know for sure but I believe that we have overcome this trouble. Don't worry, my dear," I reassured him.

"I am glad to hear that," he replied.

At last, we were clear of Romanian customs and reached the camp for refugees. We got out of the car. We looked as if we had all had a nervous breakdown. People came to us, giving a lot of presents: food, nappies, toys, clothes. I was in shock, just crying. I was almost hysterical. I could not stop thinking about the stress that we had just endured. I had saved Maxim's life and saved my family. Thankfully, we were all together.

Maxim was talking to a volunteer nearby. They discussed where we could stay and if we could live in Romania without foreign passports. When we were leaving Kharkiv, we did not get all the appropriate documents and now we were in Romania without foreign passports and any of our diplomas.

I was confused and lost, standing among hundreds of people chatting and drinking tea. They were talking about their situations and support for other Ukrainians. My mind was somewhere far away. I was just waiting until Maxim came back over.

He said, "Let's go."

I followed him into the car and we drove to our new place, a Christian church which acted as a hostel for Ukrainian refugees. When we entered the building, we saw a lot of

Ukrainian families walking upstairs and downstairs and preparing for bed. We were very hungry and we were instructed to go to the canteen to have a snack.

The Romanians were very welcoming and kind. They hugged and supported us. I was pleasantly surprised by their sincere desire to help. Their welcoming behaviour made me a bit less stressed.

Having eaten a little dinner, we went to the second floor into a huge room with a lot of mattresses on the floor with piles of bed sheets on it beside them. This room used to be a place where masses were held. There were high ceilings with big ornament windows and beautiful mosaics and paintings with Goddess characters. As it was night, I could not see the whole place.

We chose two mattresses. We put all our possessions down nearby. Lev was sleepy but crying nervously. We let Tishka out of the cage. In the room, there were a lot of sleeping people and some dogs. Tishka had never seen dogs in his life, so he was crying and hiding. Misha kept looking out for Tishka. He was afraid that Tishka would go outside and we would lose him. The entrance door was open, so Tishka really could have slipped away at any time.

Lev could not get used to sleeping on the floor. Usually, we would lull him in the stroller and after that, put him onto the bed. But now, we were in panic mode. Tired and sleepy, we were trying to make him sleep, but he was continuously crying. Tishka was also crying and trying to keep away from the dogs.

One Ukrainian woman with a strict voice said, "Do something with your naughty baby and your cat. We want to sleep!"

"What can I do?" I asked, "My son is just one year old and he is tired after the journey and our cat is just a frightened animal."

"Just shut up," she barked at us.

I left the room with Lev, sat down on the floor near the entrance and started crying. Tears ran down my cheeks, neck and chest. I was lost and exhausted. I wanted to hide from this hell world. I felt so miserable.

Maxim came up to me and tried to calm me down, "Honey, we are together. You behaved very bravely at customs. I could not act like you. You are my heroine, my saviour.'

"Thank you, my love," I said. "I am so glad that you are with us. But what can we do next? How can we live here?"

"I do not know. Let's think about it tomorrow," he said.

Suddenly, I raised my head and stared at him excitedly. I remembered that it was his birthday.

I rushed to the big room to get the kids. I took out a little chocolate cake from the bag which I had bought in Ternopil and put a candle in the middle of it. It was not too impressive for a birthday party, but it was lovely enough, presented with love and tenderness.

We were all standing in a circle in the hall with the cake in the centre. Maxim came to us and his facial expression changed. He smiled and he looked pretty surprised but very pleased.

"Happy birthday! Happy birthday!" we shouted excitedly but not very loudly. We were afraid to wake the other people in the room.

"Oh, my dear. Thank you very much. I have forgotten about my birthday. It is so unexpected," Maxim said, then hugged me.

"Children, let's sing a song and our daddy will blow out the candle and make a wish."

Maxim looked up for a minute and started blowing. In a whisper, we sang, "Happy Birthday to you! Happy birthday to you! Happy birthday, our daddy! Happy birthday to you!"

We did not have any spoons with us and it was too late to go to the canteen, so we ate the chocolate cake with our hands. We looked so funny with dirty hands eating the birthday cake together in the hall on the chair. Tishka was also with us, Annya was holding him and cuddling him, but he intended to go running. He desperately needed freedom. He was so tired from this endless travelling. His health was not very good; he had problems with his stomach. These long journeys in the cage had caused big issues for him. The poor animal was in pain and suffering.

It was about two o'clock in the morning and at last, Lev fell asleep and we could go to the big room and have the opportunity to relax. The day had been so long and unbearably hard. I did not have the energy to think about anything. I just prayed and thanked God for the day and his generous help on the border. It was a miracle, and I felt that I had been saved every time on the road. I was covered by God's hands.

Next day, I was woken up by Lev's crying and Misha, running around the room. He came up to me nervously and said, "Mum, I think Tishka has gone. I cannot find him anywhere."

He seemed very disappointed, almost crying.

"Misha, please, calm down. Give me a minute, I will help you," I told him.

I stood up with Lev and we started to search for the cat. Thankfully, people were not sleeping any more. So, we could walk near their mattresses carefully. There was a lot of furniture in the room. It was crowded with people's possessions. For one hour, we looked everywhere but there was no sight or sound of him. At last, I decided to check behind the battery on the wall. He was there, hiding from the dogs. The poor cat was stuck there and was afraid to move. I tried to lift him out but he was crying and wanted to hide again. It was so hard to explain to the animal what was going on. We loved him but we could not change our current conditions. All we could do was get used to them.

The big room, full of people and their possessions.

Later, we went downstairs to have breakfast. I met some new people from different places in Ukraine. I made new friends immediately. Grief and disaster united us. We had the same pain.

In the canteen, there were also a lot of beds for refugees. I saw little kids with a lost look in their eyes. They might have been thinking about their homes, friends. In one place, here were hundreds of broken destinies from Ukraine. It was hard to imagine how much each of them had coped with before. As I ate, I thought about them, wondering if there was anything I could do for them in this situation.

Many beds all laid out across the floor.

I finished my breakfast and went back to the room with my kids. I lay on the mattress and covered my face with my hand. I needed some time to rest.

Then, I heard a conversation between a woman and her daughter, "Alla, you spend too much time on the telephone. It is better to study English. You need it more than these stupid games."

"Mum, it is impossible. How can you think about that?"

An idea crossed my mind. 'I can help them with English', I thought. It will put them in a good mood and give them some entertainment.

I rushed back to the canteen and called out, "In thirty minutes, I will be waiting for your kids in the room upstairs. There will be a free English lesson there. I am an English teacher so I have decided to help your kids to learn some English. I think it will be useful for them in foreign countries."

My new English students

I walked around the room and invited everyone personally. At that moment, I came to the conclusion, 'If I am here, it is not by accident. I must share what I can at the place where I am now. I can teach, I can understand people and I can inspire them. So, I should do my best, even if I have no confidence in myself'.

As the room used to be a church, there were a lot of benches and I was even able to find a white board with markers. Unbelievably, it looked like a real classroom. Soon, about ten kids came and took their places.

The woman who had been talking to her daughter was very surprised with my idea.

"Wow. I was just talking with my daughter about studying English. And now you are going to teach her. Miracles happen!" she said.

"Yes, they can happen every day. It is true," I replied.

Me and my classroom.

All the kids were of similar ages, between ten and thirteen. So, it was relatively easy to give a lesson to them which I organised spontaneously. It turned out to be funny and entertaining. We threw paper balls and repeated grammar and vocabulary. We drew monsters and described them. One girl was very shy. She was afraid to take part. But I tried to involve her in the process.

After the lesson, her mother came to me and said, "Sorry about my daughter. She thinks that she is not good at English. At her school in Ukraine, she has always had bad grades."

I looked straight at the girl and said, "I want to tell you a story. Years ago, I was your age. I studied hard at school but my English was very bad. I got low grades all the time. I didn't think that my teacher would ever give me a higher grade. Soon, another teacher came and everything changed. She believed in me. She gave me extra lessons after school. She spent a lot of time checking my papers. They were full of mistakes. But I was persistent. I came home and did my homework again and again. Her belief in me and my desire to learn English helped me to progress very much." I paused and then continued, "Very soon, the situation changed dramatically. I did all my tests without any mistakes. I became the best pupil in the English class. I started participating in all language competitions. And now, I am here, teaching you. Do you know what was the secret of my success? What do you think?"

"You were clever and your talent came out, weren't you?" she replied.

"No, the secret is that we are capable of doing everything in our life. There are no limits for us. If we want to be good at something, we can always do it. We limit ourselves, close ourselves in the cage of fear. But if we decide to reach any goals, if we do not forbid ourselves to be better, we can always gain success. I was not successful in studying English, but I practiced with determination and assertiveness. I wanted to improve. I did it and you can do the same. No obstacles are ever insurmountable," I confirmed to her.

"You are right. I promise to try harder and, maybe, one day, I will speak English like you," she said.

"Of course, you will. I really believe in you," I said. "Just do it step by step and do not listen to people who doubt you."

"Thank you, Katheryna," Helen said. "I am glad that my daughter had a lesson with you. I hope your words will inspire her to be more confident. It is a pity that at school, she did not have a teacher like you."

One boy came up to me and asked, "How many lessons will we have today?"

"Just one," I answered and smiled.

"I want more lessons," he said. "They are interesting. They are not so boring like the ones at school."

At the end of the lesson, I said that the next one would be the following day at the same time. I gathered up all the papers and pens from the desks. Tishka was sitting next to the board, waiting for me.

"Tishka, are you hungry, my sonny?" I asked softly and took him with me to our place in the room.

I always called him this. I considered him to be my third son. I thought back to when Tishka came into our lives.

***

The year before, when I was eight months pregnant, suddenly, I wanted to have a cat. Before that, I had never liked cats much. But at that time, I wanted to have a little kitten. I told Maxim but he was furious.

"In a month, you are going to have a third baby. We will have a lot of fuss and having a cat will create extra duties. It is not a good idea," he said, adamant that he was right.

"But my dear, I feel that it is necessary for me and our future son," I insisted.

It took him some time to agree. I had to persuade him that I would take care of the cat and our baby. In the end, he agreed. I found a photo of a cat which I had located on the internet. I posted it on Facebook. The cat that I wanted would have to be three colours, long-haired and with white paws. I asked my friends to help me to find a cat that looked like the one in the picture.

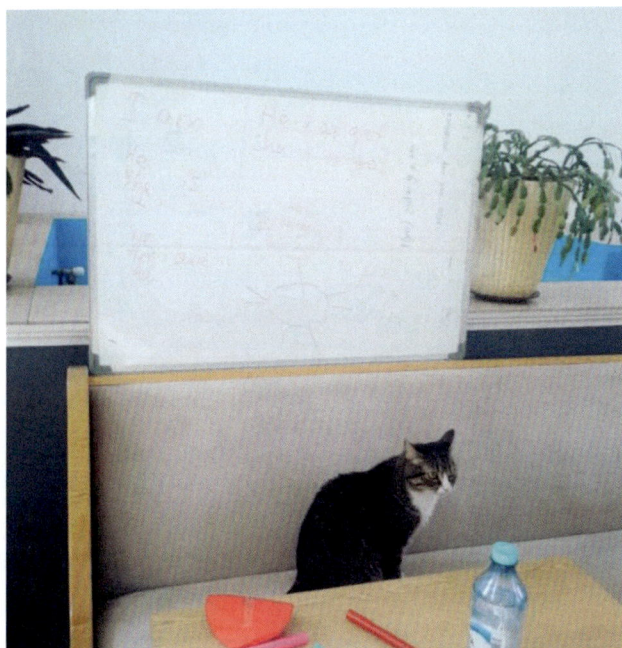

Tishka waits for me at the end of the lesson.

A hundred proposals arrived. There were a lot of cats which were looking for a new home. But they were not like the cat I had in mind. At last, I saw a photo of a little kitten who seemed similar to the one I wanted. I found the kitten's owner. She lived far away but she brought the kitten to our house by herself. We were very excited when Tishka appeared in our life. Soon after that, the following month, Lev came into this world and I had two sons, my two little kittens.

I was so glad that I managed to save Tishka in Kharkiv and now he was traveling with us. His presence in our team made me feel at home. He reminded me of our house, our city, and our happy and carefree days before the war.

I recalled our days in Kharkiv as I hugged him and headed to his food place in order to feed him.

**

Tishka was happy to have a big portion of food and then, he continued to explore the room. Fortunately, the big dogs had left and he was free to walk around.

It was a sunny day and I was sitting on my mattress on the floor. I raised my head up. I saw beautiful stained-glass windows. There were angels and saints on them. It seemed like I was in heaven. I had a magic feeling inside of me.

I thought about my purpose, asking God why I was there and what I could leave in the place. I thanked God for the shelter, and for the chance to be alive and to do something good for the world. I was shattered but at the same time, I was happy to keep going.

Suddenly, a thought came to me, 'Write.' It was like an epiphany and then, I felt calmness and bliss. Immediately, I thought about the future and I knew I had to write a book about the war, our family's experience, our trials and tribulations, and of course, my insights, feelings and knowledge gained during our journey. I would write about all the kind people we had met and been helped by. I would write about love and friendship.

The beautiful windows letting in the light.

Instantly, I stood up, took out my phone and started dictating into it, telling my story from the beginning on 24 February. I did not have any paper or pens to write with, all I had was my phone. As and when I had all the necessary writing materials, I would write everything down on paper. Now, I would do what I could with what I had.

The sun was shining through the coloured windows as I sat on the bench with my phone whispering my words into it.

There were not a lot of people in the room which was almost empty. I was with God and my new book *The Road from Kharkiv*.

At lunch, we went to the canteen. I was chatting excitedly with various Romanian people who were saying hello to me, after seeing me teach the children. I thought to myself, 'It is not so bad here. Everything will be okay'.

Suddenly, a man came up to me. He turned out to be the main person there. His name was Peter. He asked a lot of questions about me and my family. Then, he offered his help. I thanked him but I did not really know what to say.

"Where are you going next?" he asked me.

"I do not know yet. We are waiting and praying. I hope we will find somewhere to stay," I replied.

Then, he said, "Oh ... I think I can help you. Just a minute."

He called over another man who joined us.

Peter continued, "Alex, could you help this family with a place to stay? They are very nice; they have arrived recently and I know that you have a house."

"Yes, of course I can," he responded. "I have come here today to offer my house. At the moment, an English teacher from Kiev is staying there. But I think there will be enough room for everyone. It is a detached house in the city, near here."

I could not believe my ears. We were going to live in a separate house. It sounded unbelievable.

"Kate? Kate? Is it okay?" Peter asked me twice, but I was a bit numb. I was both shocked but also, very happy.

"Yes, of course. I have no words to thank you, all of you."

"Deal. I will wait for you in two hours near the entrance," Alex said and smiled. He was a tall but portly man and very kind. His eyes were sparkling and his smile was so open and sincere. When he smiled, everyone around him wanted to smile too.

"Yes, we will be on time. I will tell my family about this exciting news. They will be happy," I confirmed.

I ran back upstairs. I was eager to inform everyone about our new place. Who knows, maybe we could sleep in beds, real beds. It seemed like a miracle. I was flying like a bird.

Maxim and the boys were excited with my news, but Annya was a bit sad because she had found new friends there in the shelter.

I smile after receiving good news about a new house for us.

We started packing all our possessions and preparing for our journey to the new house. I went to the kitchen to have a snack before going and noticed the woman who had shouted at me the night before. Immediately, I thought that I had unfinished business with her. I went up to her and asked her to go to the main room. I had a surprise for everyone.

Soon, a group of women gathered near us. I took out my books with poems and offered to read them to inspire and support all of them. I sat in the centre surrounded by the women, who were all listening to me carefully.

This was one of the poems I picked to read out:

Thank you, God
And thanks for those who hurt me deeply,
They made me strong and taught me love.
You are the one who knows exactly,
What obstacles I should revive.

While I was reading these lines from my poem, I noticed that the woman who had been angry at me the night before, had started crying. Her heart was melting and I caught her eyes full of pain and at the same time, gratitude for what I was doing for her. Suddenly, she apologized and left the room.

I had little time, so I finished my little poetry concert and thanked everyone for listening. I wished them well, and to find a place where they would be safe and happy.

I said to them, "I am sure that soon you will be at the place where you should be. It is not an accident. It is your soul's destination. You might be needed there and you will need to acquire something at that place. In spite of our pain and despair, we are strong enough, because we do not give up and start our lives from scratch. So, I believe that your new life is waiting for you. Ukraine is always in our hearts but we can survive everywhere and leave a piece of our heart at any place in the world. It is vital to understand that each of us is an important part in the chain in the Universe and we should share our senses with people. Thank you for accompanying and supporting me, I have to go further. Who knows, maybe we will meet one day."

Maxim called me to tell me that we should go. I waved goodbye to everyone and went to our car. Alex was waiting. He explained to us how to get to his house. We had to follow his car. Our next stop was called Baia Mare, a few miles south of the border into Romania.

Chapter 6

Life in Romania

Spread love everywhere you go.
Let no one come to you without leaving happier
— Mother Teresa

We followed Alex, not knowing what would be ahead, just trusting him and the universe. The road was really extreme. We were going up the mountain on a serpentine. It was like a rollercoaster with very jerky turns and some steep descents too before the road would rise up again. Besides that, it was evening and it was almost dark. Maxim could barely see the road. His eyesight is poor, so he was trying to see the turns and managed to turn right or left just about on time as we kept up with Alex's car.

At last, we reached our destination. We were alive and sighed with relief. Alex got us inside his beautiful house. When we opened the door, Tatiana was standing in the hall and greeted us with a smile. I felt love and calmness there. It was such a warm feeling. I wanted to cry from happiness.

Alex's house was wonderful and cosy. There were three big bedrooms, a living room, a big kitchen and a bathroom. We felt as if we were in a dream. It was such a big contrast to the previous places we had stayed in. He gave us all the necessary things we needed such as shirts, clothes, food and toys for the children. He asked Tanja to show us everything.

That night in this house was one of the best nights during all of our wartime adventures. Maxim and I had a separate room and we slept with Lev. Misha and Annya slept in a different room.

Happy inside Alex's lovely house.

However, I found it difficult to fall asleep easily that night. I was thinking about everything that had happened to us over the last few days. A stream of thoughts in my mind never stopped flowing. I could not stop worrying and stressing about my mother-in-law and father-in-law. They lived in Mariupol which was occupied by the Russians. There had been tough fighting there. The city was only just about still standing. More than ninety percent of the buildings had been destroyed. Millions of people ended up homeless, and those who lived in their destroyed houses were without electricity, water, heating, medicine, or food. This city was truly hell on earth. People were dying from bombing, from hunger or cold in the streets. In the city, we hoped that our parents were surviving. We hadn't had contact with them since the war started. Maybe, they were dead. I did not know their situation or their fate. All I could do was wait and pray. We were now sleeping in a warm bed but for all we knew, they might have been sleeping in the cellar. My heart breaks now reflecting on these thoughts.

***

Maxim's parents were very close to me. But it took a lot of time for us to become a family. There were loads of obstacles in the beginning. When we first met, I was married to another man. It was just on paper, but I chose their son and left my husband. I fell in love with Maxim and took a risk to go to another city to be with him. It was a long story but I liked remembering it. His parents were doubtful about our relationship. But in a while, they realised how much I loved their son and how much I had to give up in order to become his wife.

When we got married and I became pregnant with their granddaughter, Annya, they accepted me into their family forever. I always felt like their daughter. I always called them my mother and father. They actually replaced my biological parents. We called each other almost every week and always bought presents on holidays for each other.

So now, when they were suffering somewhere in Mariupol, or might even be dead, my heart was broken. It looked like I had lost my parents again.

This war destroyed millions of lives. It was a knife which cut us into many pieces. Physically, I was alive, but my soul was tortured. I had no home, no information about my parents, and no hope of staying anywhere permanently. Without a doubt, this house was nice but it was given to us temporarily. We still had to think about our next steps. But I told myself to think about all of that in the morning. Now, I had to sleep. I was so tired and had given a lot of energy to people in the shelter. I needed to restore my power.

I thanked God for this day, for this miraculous house and the little ray of hope it provided for our future.

***

In the morning, our daily routine started. We had breakfast, unpacked our possessions and sorted them out on the shelves. Tanja was a very nice woman so we became friends very quickly. We spoke to her about our journey, our life in Ukraine and she shared her story with us. She was from Kiev but now she was waiting for a visa to England. Her daughters and her grandchildren were there. Her journey from Kiev had also been very hard and dangerous. They risked going out of the city at a dangerous time. Her husband had to stay in Ukraine but she crossed the border on the way to join her family in England. We supported each other and after lunch, we went for a walk together.

Baia Mare was a lovely town with narrow streets and small shops. We walked around, looking at everything. It was not a very modern place. Compared to Kharkiv, it was small. But at the same time, there were loads of entertainment places in the centre for children, cafes, restaurants and educational establishments such as schools, colleges and a university. While I was going through the town square, I felt such a pleasant feeling of peacefulness. I saw smiling people around me; Romanians were unaware of the war problems. They were happy and satisfied with their life. It was like a new world that I had accidentally fallen into.

A moment of happiness for Maxim and me.

My children saw McDonalds in the distance and started begging us to go there. We had little money but we wanted to give them a lift after so many long, hard days. We entered the restaurant and stood looking at the menu board. We tried to calculate how much we should spend based on what we could afford.

Suddenly, the cashier asked, "Excuse me, are you from Ukraine?"

We were surprised by her question. Perhaps, our appearance spoke for itself. We were wearing second-hand clothes which we had been given during our journey. Our faces were pale and thin as we had not eaten that much.

"Yes, we are from Ukraine," I replied.

She continued, "You can buy anything you want and you won't have to pay. Our organization will pay for you. We help Ukrainians. I am very sorry that in your country there is a war. So, what do you want?"

Annya and Misha eat from our surprise supply of food.

Maxim and the children happily chose everything they wanted but I was standing there crying. It really touched my heart. I did not expect that people could help us so much. I had never thought that one day, I would be given free food in McDonalds.

When we came back after the walk, Alex arrived. He brought us sacks of clothes. He let us choose what we needed. He also gave us a big packet with food. His favourite and repeated question was, "Do you need anything else?" He was like an angel amongst us. He did everything that we needed, and he did his best and tried to make our life in his house, in his country, happy, safe and calm. He seemed to feel our pain very much and helped us with an open heart. For me, it was one more situation again when PEOPLE were helping me. All the time during my journey, I was learning to receive help from people. I often thanked Alex and I even wrote him a poem:

For Alex
No words describe the help you give,
Your angel wings could cover humans,
Who lost all hopes, no place to live,
And their way's in bloody ruins.
You can feel people's pain and heart,
You know what you must say and do.
And you give light in almost dark.
You always help them to get through.
The God loves us by your kind hands,
You're his guide on duty's light.
I send you a million grateful thanks,
I'll pray for your soul every night!

I did not have any paper or pens, so I asked Tanja for a pen and found a piece of carton which she wanted to throw out as it was a part of the package of her birthday cake for her birthday which had been two days before our arrival. I wrote the text on it and presented my poem to him personally. He was overwhelmed and he started crying. It was obvious that his soul was light and his heart was so generous.

I did not have any money to repay everything people did for us but I always could make up a poem or warm words for them. It was my thank-you gift, packed with love and gratitude.

Alex. The man who helped us so much.

Alex said that we could stay in his house as long for as we wanted. The first week we relaxed. We did not plan anything as we had to recharge our batteries. We were very tired and needed time to overcome the stresses of our recent journey.

Tishka liked the house very much. When we arrived, he examined all the corners and was happy that it was an appropriate place for us to stay. He looked happy. Perhaps, it was the best place for him of all. This was the house in which he looked the most alive and playful. Looking at him, I rejoiced and dreamt of a better life.

Suddenly, my students started to write to me, asking to resume English lessons. It was unexpected. At first, I thought that it would be impossible, but then I changed my mind. On the one hand, we needed money and on the other hand, it could inspire me and provide some sense and stability to our situation. So, I agreed and began lessons almost every day. Besides that, I wrote in Misha's class chat in Viber that I could teach children English. I wanted to do something for the children in Ukraine. They were happy to accept my offer. I gave a lesson for the kids. It was for free, just my help and support for them.

I prepare to start my English lessons.

I also started giving psychological help for my friends and people from Ukraine. I thought that while I was safe, I must help those people in more difficult circumstances. They called me and I talked to them. I helped them to feel more confident and put them in better moods. Most of them started to do better in Ukraine and for Ukraine. So, my task was just to inspire people and then they continued to change their world and make a difference to others they came into contact with. I played a role like a little match which lit a flame.

Part of the money which I earned from my lessons, I sent again to Ukraine for the army and people who needed help. I felt the importance of my part in the war. My thinking was that if I was alive, and able to do something, I MUST HELP MY COUNTRY from wherever in the world I found myself. It was my national duty.

After some time in Romania, we started to think about our next step. We had to find a way to earn money and think about the kids' education. Also, our future in Romania did not look so optimistic. Alex came to us and brought up the topic of the possibility of us moving country again.

"I have some friends in Austria and they might also give you a house like this and everything you need," he began, looking at us to check our reaction to his suggestion.

"Yes, it seems like a good idea, I responded, "but how?"

He continued, "I will ask them and tell you later. I suppose it will be better for your family. Austria has a good programme for Ukrainian refugees. They help very much and I am sure you can find a better job and your kids can go to school there."

"Yes, you may be right. But it is so frightening to go to another country. It is new stress and a long journey, but I agree with you that for our kids it will be better," I said.

"Please, don't think that I want you to leave my house," he said trying to reassure us. "I just want to help you and help you find a more appropriate future. In Romania, we do not have good living conditions for you and our economy is much worse. So, you should try to find a nicer place for starting a new life. What do you think?" he asked.

"We agree with you," Maxim said. "We will wait until you get some more information."

When Alex left the house, we thought about his idea. We had been speculating about moving to another country, but we were afraid of going to an unfamiliar place without knowing anyone there.

The whole family enjoy a few rays of sun.

After we had discussed this question, many days passed. Alex helped us with everything. He took us to the shop and bought all the necessary clothes and items for our daily routine. But he did not come back to the topic of moving to Austria. We did not want to remind him but to let him bring up the subject when he had new information.

One day, we went for a walk in the centre of the town and on our way, we saw a little catholic church. I asked Maxim to wait near it and I went inside.

When I went in, I saw a big metal gate. It was closed. But I could see everything inside the church. So, I decided to pray near the door. I said everything which wounded my heart. I talked with God about our trials, my worries about the family and of course, about the war in Ukraine.

I said out loud, "My God, I do want this war to finish soon. A lot of people are dying. It is so hard to see this hell which is going on in my lovely country. The Russian army came to us and destroyed so many places, houses, and killed so many people. They do not have any compassion; they go deeper and deeper in Ukraine and destroy everything on the way. It is so hard to stay a loving person and not to hate. I do my best to save my soul. But every day, I think about it. I miss my home, my happy life in Kharkiv, and my English school. The Russians stole everything and I feel that I am empty. I do not have anything. Everything that I possessed I had to leave there. I did not bring any things from my flat. My memory is there … I am there."

I could not stop saying everything to God. I had been keeping so much inside me for so long, so at that moment, I managed to pour everything out. I burst into tears. I clung to the metal stick of the gate and slowly kneeled. I continued …

"My God, all the way I have trusted you. But this uncertainty makes me crazy. What can I do? When will we go to Austria? And should we do that? I am so frustrated and unsure of everything. I just do what I feel and take it step by step. However, it is so complicated and unbearable. I am broken.

"My motherland is Ukraine; my home is in Kharkiv. Here, everything is strange for me. I cannot feel at home here. Give me an answer. Why am I here? Please, give me any hints. I am missing my home. My home is Kharkiv."

I shouted loudly and started crying heavily.

Suddenly, I got a message, 'Your home is not only Kharkiv. Your home is the Earth, the whole planet. The world needs you'.

Immediately, I stopped crying got off my knees and stood up. I was staring at the icon with God and kept silent.

Then, I wiped my tears quickly and left the church.

Outside, Maxim and the kids were waiting for me.

"Is everything okay?" Maxim asked me, noticing my red eyes.

"Yes," I replied, "now it is okay. But I need to think about something very important for me."

We walked beside the beautiful monuments. Maxim talked to me about our English school and its future. I tried to answer him but all my thoughts were far away. I was thinking about that phrase which I received in the church. It impressed me so much and provoked a lot of reflection. The more I thought about it, the deeper I plunged into its sense. I raised my head and looked at the people around me. They did not look like strangers to me anymore. They were the people from my planet. My soul was here for some reason. I needed to trust my way and go further.

"Mum?" Annya called me and I came back to reality.

"Can we eat some ice-cream in a cafe?"

"Yes, that's a good idea," I said. "Let's go."

In the evening, we went home. I was in a good mood and was ready to do something good for others. I decided to make a live video for Ukrainians and read my poems to try to support and inspire them. I was happy to give people some of the new energy I was feeling after my visit to the church.

Annya and Misha enjoy a hot drink.

During the war, I noticed a lot of aggression and hatred among people in Ukraine. They made it very clear how much they hated the Russians. I felt the strong hate that they held in their hearts and I wanted to change it. Whenever I wrote, it was about love, forgiveness and life purpose. I explained that hate cannot beat hate, but love can beat everything. We needed to unite, be kinder, go through our obstacles and save our hearts without darkness and hatred. I even created a group in Telegram and invited those people who shared my approach and needed support.

War was such a devil's poison which entered people's souls. It was so hard not to get caught by these manipulations of the devil. Loads of Ukrainians had lost their homes, close relatives, and families. Of course, they wanted to cry and hate their enemy. But on the other hand, if we hated everybody, anybody, it would not help the situation, just worsen it. Feelings of loathing were full of very strong negative energy which could devour the person, blocking light in their hearts.

I talked to them almost every day and tried to change their reactions, to give them light and love, to support them and talk about mercy. Some of them accepted my views, but most told me "to put my rays of light in my ass!" I understood that I could not do more than I was able to do. I just shared my thoughts about love, writing positive posts and suggesting to people that they try to be kinder.

I wrote that the Russians wanted us to hate them and take revenge. But we were not like them. We were a strong and kind nation. We could love. We could love even now, during the war. It was so difficult, but I was sure we would be able to help people open their hearts. Under these obstacles, we would not be broken but evaluate our souls. It was our chance to become better.

Next day in the morning, Alex came and brought us good news.

"So, tomorrow you will go to Austria. My friend Linda will wait for you there," he informed us.

"Yahoo! Wonderful news!" I exclaimed, reacting emotionally, clapping my hands.

"We should prepare everything for your journey," he continued.

"Yes, Alex. I was thinking about it. We should do car insurance and I heard about some payment for certain roads in Europe," I said.

"You are right. Tomorrow we will arrange everything. I will help you. Don't worry," he reassured us.

"And I should fill up my car with petrol. Could you suggest any petrol stations?" Maxim asked him.

"No problem. Certainly, we will do all the necessary preparations. Now you can pack your things and tomorrow, I will come and will do everything with you before you go," Alex confirmed.

"Thank you, Alex. We are so grateful for you. You have done so much for us. What can we do for you?" I asked.

He replied, "Promise me, when I come to you in Austria in a year, you will be happy, and we will have a barbecue in your garden. I have helped you but I'm sure this kind chain will not finish. You are very good people. I was happy to do something for you."

"Thank you for these words. Yes, we will have the best and the most delicious barbecue ever," I said.

"See you tomorrow," he replied bidding us goodbye.

After he left, we started packing things. We were excited thinking about our future life in Austria. Simultaneously, another oncoming journey frightened me very much. I wondered, 'What will we do there? Where will we live?' My mind was full of worries and troubles again.

When we finished with all our possessions, we collapsed on the bed exhausted. Before we fell asleep, I talked with Maxim about our journey and our Austrian life to come. We were predicting possible obstacles and problems on the way, trying to solve them in advance.

'Tomorrow will change our life', I thought to myself.

In the morning, I got up at eight o'clock and rushed to the kitchen to prepare breakfast for all of us and cooked some food for our journey. Alex called us to inform us that he was busy with our car insurance.

We waited for him for several hours and began to think that it was too late to start driving. We were about to postpone our journey. But suddenly, he arrived and claimed that we could go then.

Even late in the day, we were ready to start. We hugged Alex and Tanja and thanked them for everything. We had lived in the house for nearly two weeks but now it was time to move on. We took a selfie of us and set off to a new country, to a new life and to new trials as we would find out, later.

Time to leave Romania for Austria. We say goodbye to Alex.

We were off and looking through the windows, saying goodbye to the Romanian town of Baia Mare, to this lovely country and its kind, open people.

It was a bit sad to leave the place where you felt love and safety. But we had made a decision and we needed to trust the proposals from the universe. Maybe, we had to be in Austria and it was our destination in more ways than one. As God said, 'My home is the earth and people need me everywhere'.

Chapter 7

Disappointment and Trials

Sometimes life takes you into a dark place where you feel it's impossible to breathe. You think you've been buried, but don't give up, because if truth be told, you've actually been planted
— *Karen Gibbs*

The journey to Austria was not so easy. Loads of Ukrainian cars were heading to and through Hungary and on to Austria. We often stopped and waited in the long, endless traffic jams. We spent a long time waiting to go through customs at the Hungarian border. At least, nearby, the Red Cross was offering food and toys for children. We were happy to have a snack because we were very hungry and tired. After a long time waiting, at last, we managed to cross. But I felt bad, I was very sick. When we left customs, I asked my husband to stop and I ran to the toilet. It occurred that I had food poisoning. I had severe pain and felt weak. It was hard for me to stand up, my legs did not obey me and I was dizzy. I wanted to go to bed and sleep but that was not possible. We had to keep going. We were not even in the middle of our journey.

It took me half an hour to recover and feel a bit better and then, I went back to the car. Lev was crying; Tishka was meowing constantly and my pain was killing me. I tried to put up with it and gritted my teeth to endure the discomfort.

After driving across Hungary and crossing the Austrian border, finally, after many hours and hundreds of miles, we arrived in Vienna. It was midnight. Everyone was deadly tired and could not move. We dreamt of finding a room and sleeping.

But it all went wrong.

We found the appropriate place but it was closed. We called Linda, whose phone number Alex had given us. But she did not answer. We were lost. We called all possible contacts to find out where we could go and stay. Then we went to another address which we got from the refugee camp but it was also closed. It was two o'clock in the morning, the children were crying from fatigue and I desperately wanted to lie down.

Luckily, we found a camping site. We almost crawled inside. When we entered, we knew that we had to do Coronavirus tests and complete various pieces of paperwork. "Oh, no," I shouted to myself.

At close to four o'clock, we were allowed to go to a gigantic room with hundreds of beds. It looked spooky and uncomfortable. We faced a very big problem with Tishka. We could not go to sleep, because the doors in this hall were open and we could not let him out of the cage. He begged us to, as he wanted to go to the toilet and walk about. Also, he was very hungry. Misha, who looked exhausted, said confidently, "I will look after Tishka. I will find a closed place for him. He is suffering. I can't sleep until I know that he is okay."

He found a place on the ground floor and let him out. My heart was broken thinking that my son was not sleeping, sitting on cold ground helping our cat. So, I went to take his place. I thought that it was better to go back to our car and sleep there with Tishka. I put him into the cage and went outside. It was dark; an unknown place. I walked beside the building, trying to find our car. But I could not locate it. I was lost.

I sat on the ground and burst into tears. There was so much pain inside me. I was angry at this country and I was angry that we made the decision to go to Austria. I was shocked with the people here, who saw our problems but did not want to help us. And I was very hungry.

After some time, I stood up and wandered back to the room. I was shattered. Maxim met me and proposed that he would go to the car with the cat; I could stay inside.

At last, I reached my bed. It was actually not a real bed, but a folding one with an artificial blanket. But that was not important. I wanted to relax. I tried to fall asleep but my stomach was rumbling and begging me for some food. In the camp, we were offered little pieces of bread with ketchup. That's all. I stood up again and went to the entrance hall to eat some of the bread. Then, I lay on the bed and very slowly, took a bite, trying to fill myself up, but it was impossible. I continued feeling hungry and my stomach continued to ache. Of course, the additional reason for my discomfort was my stomach infection. I had been vomiting during the day.

I fell asleep and despite my stomach pains, I dreamt about food. But it seemed as if just when I managed to fall asleep for a moment, Lev woke up.

My new day had begun. It was about seven o'clock. Everyone started to unpack their food packets for breakfast.

Thankfully, this crazy night had finished. But I didn't think we could stay for long. It would be impossible to overcome such conditions. It was difficult with Tishka here and I needed to calm down Lev.

When Maxim came back with Tishka, I asked him what we should do next. We called Alex and shared our news and talked about the difficulties we were experiencing. He called Linda and they advised us of a better camp in the western part of Austria. Again, we had to get on the road. It was painful even thinking about it.

Exhausted after all those hours and very little sleep the day before, we set off again to our new destination. We did not expect anything. We just hoped to get a bed and some bread.

After three hours driving, we arrived at the address which had been given to us. We saw recently built-up metal wagons for refugees. At first glance, they didn't look bad. At least it was like a real camp site. What impressed me very much was the wonderful view of the mountains. The place was magical and picturesque.

We found the head of the camp and asked him if we could stay. He was busy but quickly, he told his helpers to look after us. We were shown a small but separate room for all of us. It looked very cosy and neat. I was happy that we would have some privacy and freedom in our own space. This tiny room was like a gulp of fresh water at the end of a drought. In the room, there were five beds, one for each of us. We were really excited.

I lay on the bed and closed my eyes. I wanted to enjoy this happy moment.

The war taught us how to like small things and to value everything that we possessed. We were happy like kids when we were able to have a separate room. It was our own space, a tiny piece of freedom. This was luxury.

A woman knocked at our door and invited us for lunch. We were so happy to find out that we would eat real meals in the canteen. Immediately, we rushed to where all the people from the wagons were eating together.

We were given big portions with meat and spaghetti, and some salad. We took our seats at the table and started eating. The food tasted delicious. While I was eating my food greedily, I raised my head and looked at my children. I felt pain in my heart seeing them eat with such passion. They looked like hungry animals. My poor children. I was sorry that they had to go through this.

After a tasty lunch, we went back to our room. Obviously, that day was much better than the previous one. We rested, had a shower in the common shower room and called our relatives and friends as there was access to the internet. Some people did not like this wagon camp. It did look like it was constructed for beggars but I was happy to be able to eat, sleep and wash. At least we could meet our basic needs.

On the third day, I asked myself again what I could do here. Then, a woman came up to me and we talked about her grandson, Mike. She told me that he had lost his father and now he needed support and help. I offered to give him an English lesson to help Mike believe in himself.

Very quickly, I gathered more kids to teach, like I had done back in Romania. I found the playroom in the camp and waited for the kids there. We had a grammar lesson. Most of the kids were teenagers from ten to fifteen. Mike also came to us. The lesson started. Everyone tried to answer my questions and wrote on the papers which I had found on the floor in the room. Mike was shy but I noticed how important it was for him to do everything correctly. Several times, I praised him and focused his attention on his obvious progress.

After the lesson, I stayed with him in the room and told him personally, "You are a very smart boy."

"Thank you," he said. "Sometimes, I feel confident but every time, it's as if someone starts shouting at me to point out my mistakes."

I replied, "It is very good that you make mistakes, because they can help you to develop and study better.

Everyone makes mistakes. But you are good at languages. You have a talent."

"Really?" he said, looking surprised.

Another new class of enthusiastic English students.

I watched him going out of the room and thought how many people just needed support to help them believe in themselves. There may have been a war going on in Ukraine but in spite of this, people still needed the same basic things, especially our children.

Next day, we woke up very early, Lev was crying. We got up and went to have breakfast. He did not eat much. After breakfast, we gave him yogurt. He started crying more severely.

Suddenly, he vomited up his food. From this moment, our quiet time in the camp was over and our worries and stress about Lev began.

The whole day and all night he was vomiting and crying continuously. He did not eat anything and drank very little. Nothing helped. We gave him some medicine but his condition did not improve. The next morning, he stayed in bed. He was very weak. He did not open his eyes much. All he did was sleep most of the time.

I found the head of the camp and asked him about a doctor. He explained to me that he was busy and I should wait. But Lev was getting worse and worse. At last, I made him call the local doctor but this doctor did not want to come and help us. He said that he could not help people like us. He just recommended drinking more liquids. But this was stupid advice as Lev was sleeping all the time. His breath was getting lighter and lighter.

I was in despair. It felt like my one-year-old son was dying and nobody wanted to help.

I was standing near the office and crying. At that moment, I hated this country.

Suddenly, a woman came to me and asked me what had happened. I shared everything with her.

Immediately, she went into the office and declared firmly to the manager, "You must call the emergency services now! Quickly. If you do not do it now, you will be guilty of her son's death."

"Okay. I understand," he answered, looking confused. I saw how nervously, he tried to find the number. He called the emergency services. He said something in German which I did not understand and after finishing the call said, "The ambulance will be here in five minutes. You must go and wait outside."

"Okay. Thank you," I replied.

I wiped away my tears and ran outside.

I stood near the gate and watched the road, waiting for the ambulance. Accidentally, I heard a conversation of a young lady opposite me talking on a phone.

"You must be joking. I won't stay in this place." She said. "It looks like a place for dirty tramps. I wasn't born in a rubbish bin. I don't deserve that. Send me money and book a good room in a hotel. I will not stay here anymore."

I was listening to her and thinking about me and this girl. We were standing so close to each other and we were both experiencing pain but it was different for both of us. She was crying about her dislike of the camp and I was striving to save my child. We were each in a different universe, each with its own life and level of problems.

At last, the ambulance arrived and I waved excitedly to attract the driver's attention.

I heard again the woman next to me on the phone, "And now, an ambulance has arrived. Maybe, these dirty tramps had problems or even died. You must do something to take me out. I'm frightened!"

I ran quickly to our room with the ambulance crew. They checked the level of liquid in Lev's body. It was way too low. It was critical. They put a catheter in his vein and gave him medication. Lev lay still, without moving, looking like a plant. He was on the verge of death. He must have been severely dehydrated.

They said that we had to go to the hospital with them urgently. I collected a few things and with my sleepy, weak son, I followed the men back to the ambulance.

It seemed to me that we were driving for ages just silently sitting inside the vehicle and looking at each other. I was frustrated and scared. I just hoped that we could save him.

When we arrived at the hospital, we were taken to the office of a duty doctor. He examined Lev and gave instructions to the nurses. They started treating Lev with medicine and asked me to go to the ward.

When we were there, I put Lev on the bed and sat next to him crying. I whispered to him, "My poor son, please come back to me. I can't imagine my life without you!"

He continued to lie there with his eyes closed. Despite his stillness, I was confident that the doctors would help him. I felt trust in these kind people in white robes. I wanted to trust them. In many ways, I had no choice.

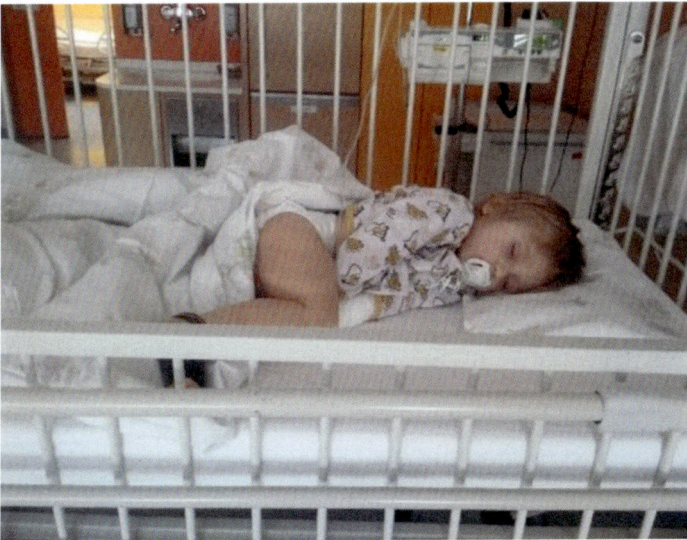

Lev sleeps in the hospital.

The ward was light, airy and very comfortable. It reminded me of a nice, one-room-flat. There was also a shower room and toilet. I looked through the window and enjoyed the view. I could see a picturesque meadow with some animals and endless green fields. It was so charming.

There was silence in the room and I prayed. I waited for Lev to awake again. I was waiting for a miracle. Then, I took my mobile phone and wrote a post in which I shared all the painful events which had happened to me. I was crying as I typed the words. My soul was eager to say everything to the world. I was so tired and weak. After having written it, I put the phone on the chest of drawers next to the bed and fell asleep.

I woke up because of Lev's crying. I jumped up instantly.

"Lev, hello. My dear. I am so happy, my boy," I said to him.

He looked at me and I listened to his voice attentively. We gazed at each other for some time and then he closed his eyes and fell asleep again.

I sent a text to Maxim to tell him that Lev had woken up briefly. I knew that everything would be okay then.

It was late evening and I was afraid to sleep. I waited.

The nurse came into the ward.

"Hello. How are you?" she asked me.

"I am okay and Lev is better. He has already opened his eyes. But not for long," I told her.

"That is very good," she said. "Don't worry. He needs more glucose. When he wakes up again, give him some sweetened water. There's a bottle with strawberry syrup."

"Thank you. I will," I assured her.

"Your boy is a real fighter and he is very handsome," she said.

"Yes, he is my angel. I love him very much," I said.

"I will come back later. You look very tired. You have to have a rest. Call me if you have any problems," she said as she left the room.

Afterwards, I was left alone with my thoughts and feelings.

I closed my eyes and remembered the day when I suggested to Maxim that we have a third baby.

***

It was the period of time when I wanted to change my life dramatically. I was planning to go to India alone to find the answers to my questions. Something was calling me there. It seemed to be the right place for me. It was called Dharamsala. I had written to a woman who I did not know well. We had seen each other once when she had arrived with a Tibetan monk in Kharkiv. When I asked her how to get to Dharamsala, she told me, "The monk Kamil is waiting for you. He remembered you and knew about your arrival." I had a lack of words. "How?" It was like magic.

"Kate, don't worry about anything. I will meet you personally and your room in the hotel will be waiting for you."

"It sounds unbelievable," I said.

"No, it just means that at last, you have found what you really need. You are following your soul. We will even organise a meeting with the Dalai Lama."

Everything was easily arranged. I bought tickets and packed my things. I was looking forward to going. But suddenly, quarantine was announced and all our flights were cancelled. I was so disappointed. Every day, I checked the status of the flight and believed that the situation would change but miracles did not happen.

I clearly remembered 24 March when I came into the bedroom where Maxim was resting and suggested, "Let's have a baby?"

"What?" he asked me looking amused.

"I can't fly to India. Today is the day of the flight ... and ... I thought ..." I murmured quietly, "Why can't we have a third baby?"

He looked at me but did not answer. I kissed him and smiled shyly.

"Maxim, I love you. It is a spontaneous decision but I feel that I want it. I really feel it. I want to have one more son.

Then, I kissed him again with passion. And he answered me. And that night became one of the most memorable nights in our life. Our intimacy that night was like a spiritual exchange. I was so happy and blessed. Our souls merged in one. In the end, we fell asleep in each other's arms.

Next morning, I was worried about the previous night. But then, I thought that I could not be pregnant after just one attempt. I had had experience with Misha and Annya, when I could not get pregnant for several years.

'It was such a spontaneous decision and I am pretty sure that I will not be pregnant,' I said to myself.

After a month, I knew that I was pregnant with Lev. I did not go to India on 24 March but my Indian miracle appeared in my body. While I was pregnant, I changed very fast. I became a writer and produced the first and second of my three books published in Ukraine. I changed my career and became a psychologist. I read a lot of books about philosophy, Indian wisdom and a lot of other spiritual literature. All the time, I felt the presence of my unborn baby; I felt his soul. He was changing me and my life.

Lev was born on 12 December. It was a real miracle for me. When I saw him for the first time, I realised how strong my love for him was. And since his birth, I could not stop doing new things. We studied together coaching for the purpose of life and I managed to provide more than fifty consultations with him on my knees. Lev gave me so much energy to make unreal improvements in my life. I was really happy that I had not gone to India but had suggested to Maxim that we have a baby.

***

I opened my eyes which were wet from tears and looked at my son in the bed. He looked like an angel. I felt a lot of love and gratitude to God that he presented me with this little miracle. And then, exhaustion overtook me and I fell into a deep sleep.

In the morning, I woke up very early. My nervous system was very poor. Since the war began, I had slept badly. I was lying in bed and thinking about when we would leave the hospital. For several days, I called Linda but she did not answer. Alex had given us her contact details and promised that she would help us in Austria. Camping was the first stage which we had to go through. After that, Linda should have taken us from the camp and taken us to a new house. I sent her a dozen messages but there was silence. At last, I got a message, "I did not promise you anything. In this camp, you will get proposals. Wait for them ..."

I was frustrated. We were in the hospital in Austria and the only person who had promised us to help declined my calls and could not help us at all. I felt I was being set up. I did not know what to do next. I did not want to disturb Alex anymore, as he had done a lot in Romania. I had to come up with a new way to survive in Austria.

Meanwhile, Maxim called me while I was crying, sitting on the bed and staring at the phone, "Kate, how is Lev?" he asked.

"Amazingly, he is better. How are Misha and Annya?" I replied.

"They are also okay but missing you and asking about you ..." he told me.

"I want to come back as soon as possible, Max," I said. "What can we do? Linda does not want to help us. We've been let down."

"We have been offered a hotel in the west of Austria. But we would have to leave Tishka. What should I answer?" he answered.

"Tell them 'No', we will never leave our cat. He is a part of our family," I said.

"Okay. I will refuse," he confirmed. "But where will we live? After you come from the hospital, we will be on the streets. We should make a decision now."

"I see ... I feel lost. I need time to calm down and think over it again, being quiet with a clear mind, without emotions," I explained.

"Don't worry, honey. Everything will be fine," he reassured me. "We will find a solution to this problem. We have overcome so many obstacles and survived in such dangerous situations, and now we will do it again. I am always next to you."

"Yes, we should trust everything that God gives. Kiss Misha and Annya from me," I told him.

"Bye. Soon we will see each other," I said, finishing the conversation. As I did, I started crying. I prayed and asked for help. I tried to find options in my mind for finding a place to live. But there were no ideas.

When I calmed down, I decided to go on Facebook and I was shocked. There were hundreds of messages from different people. It was such a massive reaction after my post the previous day. I was pleasantly surprised. 'What is going on?' I wondered.

I did not know who I should answer first. There were so many different options. Suddenly, one of my friends from Kharkiv called me, "Kate, are you in the hospital now?"

"Yes," I answered reluctantly, not knowing why she was calling me.

"We have a flat for you and your family. After the hospital you can go there," she said.

"It sounds unbelievable. It can't be true," I blurted out.

"But it is true. Give my number to your husband, I will tell him everything," she confirmed.

I hung up and I looked happily at the sunny meadow through the big window. A new day had come and we had a new hope!

At the same time, Lev opened his eyes and smiled at me. He tried to stand up and asked to eat. I fed him with the food which we were given in the hospital. He ate it with relish. I was so happy to see my child alive and cheerful.

He did not want to stay in bed with catheters. He jumped up and tried to leave the ward. He wanted to go home. I was standing near him and helped him not to get tangled up.

When the doctor came into the ward and looked at Lev, he was astonished.

"Oh, someone wants to go home. It is really a miracle how your son has recovered so quickly," he observed.

"Yes, I am also very surprised. It is a wonder! He can walk and he is eager to leave this place," I confirmed.

"And he is right. Your analyses are good. You can go home now!" the doctor agreed.

"I can't believe it! Thank you. I should call my husband. There is so much good news at the same time. Thank you, doctor," I said to him.

I was so excited looking forward to going to a new flat.

Unfortunately, my joy did not last so long. Maxim called me and had to give me some bad news. He said that we could not go to the flat right then, but only in a month. We would need a place to live in until then.

I answered, "Okay." Sadly, we had no other choice.

I collected our things and waited for Maxim. He would collect us from the hospital by car. I wrote some words on the napkin for the nurses and the doctor in three languages: English, German and Ukrainian. I wanted to leave my love and gratitude for them.

Then, I took Lev and my bag and went outside to wait for Maxim. I was walking along the long corridors in the hospital and thinking that it was not like the real world. It seemed to me that I was in a film and I was the main protagonist. 'Will this adventure finish once or will we move from one place to another all our life forever?' I wondered.

When I met Maxim, I hugged him and kissed him. I was glad to see him again. I saw the kids in the car and could not understand why they were there with him, not in the camp.

"Will we go back to the camp?" I asked suspiciously.

He smiled.

"Max, what's going on? Explain to me," I insisted.

"We are going to a new house. Anne, your friend found another option for us. And in half an hour, we will be there," he revealed.

I jumped on him and hugged him tightly.

"A miracle! Again and again," I shouted with a smile.

I raised my head up and said with love, "Thank you, God."

Chapter 8

Hard Times in Austria

Nobody is exempt from the trials of life, but everyone can always find something positive in everything even in the worst of times
— Roy T. Bennett

Soon, we were heading towards our new house. Everything was so amazing that I was afraid to believe it was happening. I wanted to be sure that it was not a joke. I knew that I would only be more confident when we actually arrived and could stay at this new place definitely.

Everyone was so tired. We all sat silently in the car. We did not have the energy to discuss anything. We were as tired in mind as we were in body.

At last, we reached our destination. We stopped near an old house with a pretty bench opposite. We got out of the car and saw Anne, who was running towards us. She hugged me tightly. I wanted to cry.

"Anne, thank you," I said. "I am so grateful to you. I don't have words to describe my feelings."

"Kate, all your trials are over," she replied. "You can live in this house. A new happy life can start now."

She pointed towards the front door. It was a really old house, but I was so delighted. It seemed so cosy and comfortable after all our adventures. A lot of people were cleaning and preparing it for our arrival. It transpired that nobody had lived there for five years. A very old man, the owner of the house, had died and it had been left empty since then. The owners of the house were Bertha and her husband Martin, who were nice, kind people. They also came to greet us.

I liked the inside of the house. Its energy was so beautiful. When I came into our bedroom, I saw a big picture of St. Magdalena and five angels. It was a sign for me. At that moment, it was the place where I wanted to live.

I did not have the energy to do anything. I just wanted to go to the bedroom and fall asleep. But with all my strength, I tried to answer everyone's questions and say thank you.

In the evening, Maxim and Anne went to the bus stop to fetch our future housemate, Lily, and her two kids. I was happy to meet her. It would be nice to live together and be friends, sharing our pain, our experiences and the duties looking after the house.

I prepared her room for her arrival and waited for them to come with anticipation.

When Lily came into the house, she looked very sad. She went around the house and concluded that it was awful. She was frightened and wanted to go home. She started crying. I tried to comfort her but she did not calm down. I understood what stress she had gone through so I did not persist in trying to raise her mood at that time.

I was very tired and I wanted to sleep. My body did not want to move anymore.

In the morning, we met in the kitchen, but Lily did not want to chat. Her children were crying and she was quite nervous.

Anne sent us an address where there was a club for refugees. People could get clothes there, eat and find support.

"Misha, Annya, can you stay at home and we will go to get some food for us. Look after Tishka and be careful. Don't go anywhere. Unfortunately, we can't take you, because our housemate Lily needs to go with us in the car," I told them.

"But mum, we are hungry," they said.

"I am sorry, we can't take you. We have to go with our housemate. But I promise, we will bring some food for you," I said trying to reassure them.

Anne wrote me a message in the morning, that I must help Lily, look after her and do everything to make her happy. I agreed to this request but honestly, I needed help too. After the situation with Lev and all our trials, I was extremely weak. Every time I made an effort to do anything, the activity was quite hard for me. I really had to force myself.

We went to another city called Neusiedl am See with Lily and her children, to the address we were given by Anne. There were a lot of Ukrainian people there. Some were choosing clothes from the bags, some were eating, and most of them were chatting and exchanging news with each other.

We chose some clothes for ourselves and our children and sat at the table to eat spaghetti and sausages. For me, the food was so delicious. I wanted to eat another portion but I was too shy to ask for more.

I was surprised to see a lot of acquaintances from back in Ukraine. They came up to me and hugged me.

"Kate, we are so happy to see you," they all said.

Most of them were people who came to my poem performances in Kharkiv, who considered me as an idol of optimism and wisdom. But at that moment, I did not look either wise or optimistic. I looked very thin and exhausted with grey sacks under my eyes and trembling hands. Since the war had begun, I had lost weight. Lack of food and the road trip had really affected me.

We finished eating and were planning to go when suddenly my husband beckoned me, "Kate, I regret to inform you but I must ..."

"What has happened?" I said panicking. My body started shaking violently.

"Tishka has died ..." he said.

"What?" I shouted. I could not believe my ears. I fell on the ground and cried like a baby.

'My cat, my Tishka ... How come? You were with us all this way. You came into all the houses and flats with us, you suffered with us, you fought with us. I risked my life to save you. I could have died, but I wanted to take you from danger. I love you so much. You were like a baby to me. How come? It is so difficult to believe this news'.

Maxim continued, "Kate, the situation is very bad. Misha and Annya are weeping. As I understand it, Misha saw how Tishka had been killed by dogs from the neighbourhood. And now, he is in shock,"

"Let's go," I said to Lily and we went to our car. Tears continued running down my cheeks. I could not stop them. I was already grieving.

Lily had to come back with us, because we had the car and could take her back home. She was unhappy to go so early because she wanted to stay longer there.

When we were sitting in the car and were ready to go, she asked me a question, "I need a cigarette. Could you help me buy some?"

I did not answer. I was crying and thinking about my kids. What are they feeling now? I could not even imagine. It was so hard to accept the news. They had witnessed this awful situation. At that moment, I was angry that Lily did not understand our feelings and was asking such questions. But she had her own pain to deal with which I understood.

Having arrived, I saw my children in despair, crying in the living room. Annya was sitting on Bertha's knees and hugging her and Misha was hiding his face in the corner of the sofa. I quickly jumped on the sofa and held them against me.

I was stroking their heads and repeated the words, "My poor kids ... I am next to you ... I love you ..."

Misha described what had happened. "Mum, two big dogs attacked Tishka. He did not understand what was happening. He just stood still. What a silly cat."

"I see, my son, I see ..." I said.

"Mum, Annya is guilty," he continued looking at her angrily. "I asked her to call for help. But she stood still," Misha cried through the tears.

"Misha, it is not her fault. Nobody is guilty here. It just must have happened."

I said these words and burst into tears. I saw a cat's body on the sofa. My heart broke.

Tishka was lying there looking like he was resting peacefully ... He looked so beautiful. I felt such deep love for him at that moment.

Annya started to speak. "Mummy, I was afraid and frustrated. I did not know what to do. I saw Tishka running into the garden and then he slipped into the hole in the wall. This hole led out into the neighbourhood. I called him back but he did not return. I called Misha to help me. He was on the other side of the fence. Sorry, mum ..." she tried to explain.

"Annya, don't say sorry. You are not guilty."

"No, she is," Misha contradicted me again. "She should have called me earlier. She lost time. I will never forgive her."

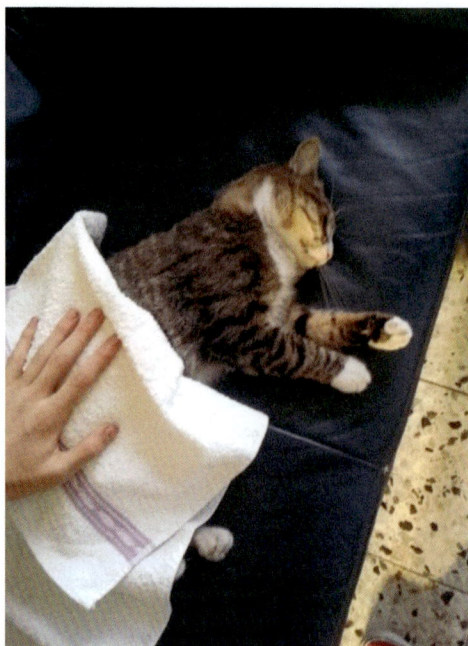

Our dear Tishka looking like he was sleeping.

I understood Misha's feelings, because he loved Tishka so much. All the way from Kharkiv, he carried him on his knees. The cat's cage was incredibly heavy but he never complained. He was suffering severely because it pressed his knees and the cat was crying all the time and moving inside it. But patiently, he looked after it all the way for all of those many hours.

The incident happened in front of his eyes. He told me the whole story later. It turned out that when Misha came to Anny when he heard the two big dogs were attacking Tishka. It was too late. Misha jumped over the fence, tearing his socks. He had not put on his shoes when he heard Annya's voice. But when he found the cat, it was almost dead. He threw himself at the dogs and scared them off so they wouldn't rip Tishka's body apart. He lifted Tishka and began running around the neighbours to ask for help.

He shouted, "Help! Help! Someone, help!"

He hoped for a miracle. At last, Bertha, noticed him and came to help. He was in despair when he realised that Tishka had died. Nothing could help him anymore.

Suddenly, Annya said, "We must bury our cat. We need a grave for him. Papa, can you do it?"

Maxim agreed with her suggestion and went quickly to the yard to dig a hole. Annya stood up, wiped away her tears with her sleeve and said bravely, "I will carry his body to the hole."

"Annya, it is not a good idea. I can do it or your father can," I objected.

"No, I want to do it. He was my friend," she insisted bravely.

She came up to the sofa where he was lying and took his dead body. Then she walked slowly towards the grave as if it was a funeral procession. Step by step, she approached Maxim who was waiting in the yard. She put Tishka's body carefully into the hole and said, "My little cat, thank you for everything you've done for us. I will always love you and remember you."

"Let's say something good about Tishka," I suggested. "Which good memories do you have about him?"

Misha began. "He was very kind. He always used to come to my room and lie near me. My mood was always raised and I cuddled him. He was on my knees all our way from Kharkiv. He was constantly crying and felt so much pain in the cage but he was struggling with his pain and waited for freedom. He never did naughty things. I loved him so much." After he finished speaking, Misha started crying again.

I was next. "I remember a day when I was sitting in the living room and crying. I was sad about something. Tishka came to me and tried to lick the tears from my cheeks. After that, he sat down near me and put his paws on my hands. In such a way, he supported me and it looked like he was saying, 'I love you. I am next to you. Everything will be okay.' I definitely know he loved me very much. He was always near when I needed some help." I finished my speech and also cried.

"He was a cool boy. It is very sad to lose him," Maxim said succinctly but sincerely.

When Annya's time finally came, she could not say anything, but her face said everything. She was suffering inside. She just said, "Papa, cover him over."

We looked at Tishka for the last time and said goodbye to him. He was our family member and our friend who was more than a simple cat; he was an integral part of us. While Maxim was covering him with earth, we stood around him crying. It was unspeakably painful for all of us. Later, Maxim set a tombstone for his grave and Annya planted beautiful flowers on it. One day, I noticed a little piece of paper stuck in the earth near his grave with words by Annya, 'I love you, my little kitten and miss you so much'.

It was obvious that Misha and Annya had psychological trauma and they needed some help from a specialist. It was too hard to overcome all these events, especially for children.

We were in grief all the time. I could not move normally. It required a lot of effort to do anything. But the next day, Anne and her friends came to our house to deal with registration questions for us and Lily. I cleaned the house and cooked some food.

All the people were sitting in the kitchen discussing the current situation. Lev was continually crying and Lily's children were also following her around and shouting all the time. I pretended to be okay, but actually I was almost falling apart. I was eager to fall asleep. I was exhausted and shattered. I was counting the seconds until I could be on my own.

At last, I was alone in my bedroom, I closed my eyes and again started crying thinking about Tishka. I kept my pain inside when I was among people. But when I was on my own, I allowed myself to cry. I felt so lost in a foreign country. Recently, Lev had nearly died and now, Tishka was gone. There was no news about my parents from Mariupol either. Perhaps, they were dead already. The war had stolen so many things from me.

We were offered an opportunity to take Misha to a psychologist to overcome his trauma and help him to get better. We went together: Misha, Annya and me. We all needed help. When we came to the psychologist, we sat and said nothing. Each of us was hurting so much.

"What do you feel after this accident?" the man asked us.

"I think we are guilty that Tishka died. Especially Annya," Misha said.

He was talking calmly and quietly but it was obvious that he was furious inside. He wanted to shout at all of us. He continued to accuse Annya of the cat's death.

"I am very sad," Annya said, "but he is okay now. I had a dream that he was in the sky and soon, he will have a new body. It will be a person. He served us very well. So, now he deserves a better life."

Everyone was surprised by Annya's words and looked at each other with wide open eyes.

Annya was always an extraordinary girl. She looked and behaved as though she knew more than we did. Later, she said that the war would last for two years and we had to put up with it and build up our life in Austria.

The psychologist also asked me about my feelings and I started to say a stream of words about all my past events, about my pain and uncertainty and certainly, about my love for Tishka.

"Tishka was with us all the way. He was our guide who accompanied us from Kharkiv to Austria. In all the places where we stayed, he made us think of home. It helped us not to be desperate. Perhaps, he died to make us stop here and start our new life. I miss him so much. He realised his big mission for all our family. He saved us and sacrificed his life for our future.

Visiting the psychologist helped us a little to overcome our grief and gradually, our state of mind returned almost to normal.

The beautiful lake at Podersdorf.

The first few days in the new place were hard for me. I was devastated and yearned for my home city. But every day,

I tried to think positively. I tried to find little rays of happiness in the darkness.

Podersdorf was a beautiful village. I liked the lake there. It was so tranquil, filling me with energy and enjoyment. I was fond of water, so living near a lake seemed to be a perfect option. I found out there was an old church in the village and I started to go there several times a week to be alone and pray. God helped me and gradually, I felt that my soul was being treated.

I was so grateful to the owners of our house, Bertha and Martin, who surrounded me with love and care. I expressed them my love and gratitude whenever I could. I wrote a poem in German, though I did not know this language at all:

Für Martin und Bertha
Martin und Bertha, danke schön
Für Ihre Unterstützung und Liebe.
Wir hatten Tränen und Depression,
Aber Ihr habt uns einen Traum gegeben.
Ihr Zuhause ist schön und geliebt,
Und Ihr seid so nette Menschen.
Wir säen Gutes in dieser Welt.
Wir werden Ihre Hilfe nie vergessen.

I cooked pies and did my best to be their nice, Ukrainian guest. For me, it was vital to give them everything that they deserved for their generosity. I remember the day when they gave me a bicycle to ride. It was very cold and rainy, but I was excited to try to ride it. I hadn't been cycling for over twenty years. It was so funny to be back on a bike, as I had forgotten how to ride. I fell every time when I stopped. But then, I remembered how to do it and I flew along the narrow streets with a big smile on my face. It was raining and the wind was blowing strongly. I felt happiness and freedom.

My children went to local schools and soon, Lev started visiting a kindergarten. Everything seemed to be going in the right direction. However, the relationship with our housemate Lily was not warm. She did not want to be close friends, but I tried to understand her state. She was alone in Austria, with little children and so much stress. She needed more time, perhaps.

I become a cyclist again.

Nevertheless, I tried to open my heart to her every day. I wanted to love her in spite of her coldness. I presented my books to her and offered to speak about her sense of life. Step by step, she opened her heart a little. She said that I behaved like a mother to her; that I was teaching her.

One day, she came up to me and admitted that when she had first arrived, she had not felt right. She said sorry for everything. She promised to change her behaviour and I witnessed the change. She started cooking, cleaning the house and she smiled more often. We had days when we were happily chatting and discussing common topics. Gradually, I found more beautiful features in Lily and started to love her.

Once, her daughter became ill. She had a high temperature and was walking around the house crying all the time. After a while, her three-year-old son started vomiting and Lev picked up this stomach virus. I was so frightened. The situation from before was repeating itself again. Lev had a high temperature, up to forty at one point. He also had sickness and diarrhoea. I was so afraid that Lev would have to go to hospital like before.

Unfortunately, her son became worse and worse. His state was critical. We called the emergency services and Lily went to hospital with her children. I helped as much as possible, in spite of the fact my son was very ill too. I often ran to Bertha's husband to help her and her son and translated Lily's words as she did not know English at all. I did my best to give her a helping hand.

When she went away, I ran to the church. It was raining heavily and a strong wind was blowing. I approached it thinking how strongly I would ask for my son's good health. I did not want to go to hospital with Lev again and have the same experience as before. When I arrived, I sat near the cross of Christ and I thought, 'God, you always help me. I wanted to ask not for my son Lev, but now I want to ask for Lily's son. He needs your help more. Please, give him a miracle. I want him to be healthy. What about Lev and me? I trust you. I am sure that you will make a wise and fair decision about us. You know better what we need and you will do the best for us. Let it be as you wish'. I finished my prayer and started crying. I felt that I had done the right thing but I was so sad and worried about Lev. I had given my wish for Lev to Lily's son.

When Lily and the children were taken to hospital, I also packed all our things in case we had to go too. Lev was also becoming worse and worse. I waited nervously. Then, suddenly, Maxim proclaimed, "I will try to treat him as I think fit. Maybe, you won't have to go to the hospital. Trust me, please."

I relied on him and did everything he said. After a day of careful attention and care by Maxim, a miracle occurred and Lev started to feel better. His temperature fell and he stopped vomiting.

It was the first day that our life began to get back to normal and Lev was almost okay. Then, I received the message from Lily, "Kate, I will not come back to the house. Anne found a better option for me. Can you help her to gather my possessions? Thank you for everything."

In the afternoon, Anne came to collect Lily's things. She cleaned her room. I did not have time or energy to clean the whole house. I was very tired after a week of hardly any sleep while Lev was sick.

The next day, Anne texted me a message that the illness of Lily's children could be the result of untidiness. It was so painful to hear that. Anne did not ask me anything about Lev and his condition. But I was not offended by her as she had saved me and had done a lot for me. She was a kind person and wanted to help all Ukrainian refugees. I owed her a lot and would never forget her help to me and my family. I just agreed with her. God knows exactly who was right or guilty.

When people accuse us of something that we did not do, there's no sense in proving our truth. The truth is obvious for the sky and for us, so it is better to allow people to think what they want and we should continue moving forward.

After a while, we had a new housemate. Her name was Elena. She came with a twelve-year-old daughter. When they arrived, Elena also seemed unhappy. On the first day, she walked around the house and did not talk to me. I tried to have contact with her but she was deep in her thoughts and worries. I decided to give her time to overcome her stresses and to speak to her later.

Next day, Bertha came to us and explained that I should be a better housemate. Before that, Bertha had always been kind to me, but after Elena's arrival, Bertha's behaviour changed dramatically. We were not close friends anymore and I did not understand the reason.

I tried to be friendly with Elena. We were going to live together, so we needed to try to get on. The situation with Lily taught me a lot, so I did my best to spend quality time with Elena.

Every day, I found little positive things and shared my love with people around me: with my family, Elena, Bertha and our other beautiful Austrian friends.

Once, a woman appeared at my doorstep. Her name was Jacqueline. She had heard about me and my spoken English. She needed someone as a volunteer-translator. Some Ukrainian families and orphans were going to arrive and she needed me to translate her words and to support the Ukrainians.

Having heard about orphans, I was so happy. In Ukraine, I had been helping orphans a lot. For me, it was real happiness to be among such kids. They were so unique and special, with angelic hearts. I accepted her proposal with enthusiasm. It could take my life back to how it used to be and make some sense again for me.

From that day on and for several months, I did volunteer work in the hotel where more and more Ukrainian refugees were arriving. And my relationship with Jacqueline was turning into a strong friendship. She also had three children like me. Every time, she knocked at my door and left something near the door on the doorsteps. She was like my angel.

It was good to help the orphans and other refugees.

I helped a lot in the hotel and spent most of my time with Jacqueline. I was excited to help the orphans and other Ukrainian refugees.

Every week, I offered them my free English lessons. It was not so easy to spend a lot of time in the hotel, because I had my family duties and my work. But I felt that I wanted to help Jacqueline and the Ukrainians. I even organised a performance of my inspirational poems for them. I was washing over them my pure love and sincere care.

For the performance, I put on a white dress which was given to me by Jacqueline, invited all the hotel people into a big room and turned-on classical music on my phone. There were not just adults but also teenagers, most of whom had very difficult lives as orphans or had been adopted. They were listening attentively to me and asked a lot of questions.

I wanted to support them and talk about the meaning of their lives.

After my performance. It was a happy event.

I recommended that in spite of the war, we should focus on our role in this world scenario. We were not here accidentally. Each of us was an important part of a long chain of humanity. Chatting with each other and helping each other, we could realise our sense; we could influence the world around us.

We make waves which go further and further. I suggested that they were not useless or invaluable in Austria, but here, because they needed to be here. I didn't know everyone's exact task, but I was sure it existed. If people's circumstances were not right for them, they should not give up but seek to find something more appropriate. It was their chance to start life from scratch; to try something new that they might have always wanted to do. Their lives were continuing. They shouldn't wait until life was better and easier but try to make things happen. Always, each person should believe in themselves.

After my performance, I came home but I kept getting messages from the people in the hotel. They asked me to send my books and to give them advice.

Time passed and Elena and I became closer. We went to the lake together. I did a photo session with her. She was so surprised by how beautiful she was in the photos. She had some complexes because of her body but I saw her beauty and wanted to visualise her strengths through the medium of the photographs.

Once in the evening, I read some poems for her from my books. She started crying. I hugged her and supported her.

I said, "I believe in you. Don't give up."

I kept trying to do good things for her: I helped her with school for her daughter, helped with work. She did not speak English, so she needed me as a translator.

I was filling my life with positivity. One day, I started to dream about the future. From Kharkiv, I had taken a little box presented to me on my birthday by my friend Natasha. One evening, I decided to write my little dreams on tiny pieces of paper and put them in this box. One of the dreams was to live in a beautiful house with a bathroom with lilies. I do not know why I wrote it. It would be like a clue for me.

Everything was going well when suddenly, Jacqueline informed me about something very important, "Kate, an elderly woman in my street asked me about Ukrainians who needed a house to live in and I remembered you. I know that living with housemates is not convenient and I notice that you sometimes look unhappy. In this new house, you will be able to live alone without anybody else. What do you think?

"It is ... It is great!" I exclaimed.

Inside of me, my emotions erupted both from surprise and excitement. I had never dreamt about such a thing happening.

Every day, I was pleased with everything that I was given. And I always accepted with gratitude all the minor gifts from God.

"So, I will go to see the house and send you photos later," she concluded.

"But Bertha ... What can I tell her?" I asked. "She has given me so much ..."

"We will go to see her together and discuss it. I am sure she will understand. But such a chance is unique. It would be silly to reject such a proposal," she replied.

"Of course, It is a chance in a million. Thank you, my angel. It is very important for me," I said enthusiastically.

"You are welcome. I am always ready to make your life happier," she said.

This news about living separately in a new house improved my mood very much. All that day, I was delighted and I was kinder and friendlier to all the people around me. I told the news to Maxim. He was speechless and very surprised.

Later, we received photos from Jacqueline. It was not just living on our own as a family and apart from other people, it was an unforgettably amazing house, very modern, with a big garden and three bedrooms. And the most important thing was that there was a bath.

Without any hesitation I called Jacqueline, "Yes, I'm ready to move," I informed her "and we will speak to Bertha."

"Kate, the house is incredible. It is a dream house. You are so lucky," Jacqueline confirmed.

"I am lucky because I have such a friend like you," I said.

"Kate, sorry, but I cannot come to Bertha now, only in three days' time. Can you wait for me?" Jacqueline asked.

"Of course, I will," I confirmed.

"See you on Monday, Kate," Jacqueline said, ending the call.

A lot of thoughts were going around and around in my mind. I thought about what I would say to Bertha and if I was behaving badly towards Elena.

For three days, I worried about the oncoming conversation. I loved Bertha and I felt warmth towards Elena and her daughter. But I could not miss this chance.

At last, the day arrived and Jacqueline and I went to Bertha's house. I had prepared a long speech, but when I saw her, I burst into tears and hugged her tightly.

"Kate, what's happened?" Bertha asked me.

"Jacqueline has found a separate house for our family and I accepted her proposal. But it means that I will have to move from your lovely house."

"My dear Kate, you shouldn't cry. Everything is okay. I understand you and of course, this is a very good opportunity for your family," Bertha assured me.

"And we can still meet, have barbecues and do a lot of things together, can't we?" I said.

"Of course, without a doubt," she confirmed.

Jacqueline was chatting with her in German. It looked like they were discussing the details of registration and some common questions.

We finished our conversation and went outside. Standing in the garden, I looked at her with appreciation and said, "Ich liebe dich."

It was truly a stone from the heart. The next day, I spoke with Elena and surprisingly, she also reacted very positively. I was happy knowing that my decision did not hurt anyone.

For two days, I cleaned the house and prepared to move to the new one. On the last day, I was so exhausted. I was almost falling asleep with fatigue. But I promised to clean everything in our rooms. While I was cleaning, Elena was next to me. We were chatting in a friendly way and I was opening my heart to her, revealing my difficult past experiences. I was so full of love and tenderness to her that I ran to the shop and bought a bunch of roses, wrote kind words in the postcard and put my book, *I Present You My Wings and Start to Live* on the pillow in her room. She spotted my present and was so happy and joyful. Her eyes sparkled.

At the end of the day, we said goodbye to Elena and moved to our new house which was about ten minutes from Bertha's. I was so tired that I did not wait until Bertha came to say her goodbye to her and to show her our rooms. Later, I realised that this had been my big mistake.

Chapter 9

A New House and Hopes for the Better

The greatest glory in living lies not in never
falling, but in rising every time we fall
— Nelson Mandela

When we arrived at our new house, we were greeted by Marta and Franz, a beautiful and charming elderly couple who were living nearby. They were in charge of the house. The real owner, Gerhard, was living in America but he came to the house from time to time on holiday.

When we went inside, we realised that it was better than we had expected. It really was the house of my dreams. I could not believe my eyes. I raised my head and said very loudly, "THANK YOU, GOD!"

I was excited looking into each room and I kept sighing in admiration. It was almost as if I was sleep-walking in a beautiful dream. Could I really be about to live in such a house with no stress and only peace and quiet? After our tough experiences, I was afraid even to think about such a possibility.

Though I was exhausted, I managed to unpack all the bags and to sort out all our possessions. I was eager to feel relaxed and to make a start living in this new house.

Before bed, I wanted to do an important thing: to take a bath. I had been waiting for this moment for ages. Throughout our journey so far, bathing had been difficult. In Bertha's house, the water in the taps was cold and I had to boil water in saucepans to take a shower. But now, I had a chance to be in paradise. I filled up the bath and slowly lowered myself into it. I closed my eyes and my life seemed to stop. It was a time for recharging, restarting and resetting. I was flying somewhere far from the earth, high in the sky. I was suspended, feeling emptiness and quietness.

Suddenly, I opened my eyes and looked at the tiles in the bathroom. They had white lilies on them. At once, I remembered my magic box and the dream wishes I had written on the pieces of paper in Bertha's house, including one wishing for a bathroom with lilies. And now, I was the witness of a real miracle. The same white tiles and a house of my dreams. My life was improving and my dreams were coming true. I was so excited and content at that moment. It was like magic. But I knew that it was certainly God's hand.

After our arrival in the new house, I experienced problems with my health: no doubt caused by the stressful situations and hard work we had been through. I had high blood pressure and my right eye was pulsating intensively. I could barely walk and I spent almost all my time in bed. I even cancelled all my lessons, which I only ever did in emergency situations.

Maxim worried about me. On Sunday, he decided to organise a family outing. He wanted to make me happier and took us all to a museum in another town.

It was a sunny and beautiful day. I was full of anticipation about having a good time with my family. When we arrived at the parking zone near the museum, a woman ran towards us shouting excitedly. She might have noticed our Ukrainian number plates on the car.

"Ukrainians. Such good luck," she said.

When she looked inside the car, she exclaimed, "You are Kate. I know you. I subscribed to your page on Facebook and I am your fan. You are my inspiration."

I was pretty surprised and delighted to know that the Ukrainians in Austria were reading about me and that I was inspiring them.

We went to the museum. It was a huge installation of an ancient Roman city with old Roman houses, other monuments and city structures. I took a lot of wonderful photos and soon my energy started coming back again.

'Maybe, my life will be without stress and I will have a chance to be happy again ...' I thought to myself as we walked around.

In the museum, I met a pleasant couple from Ukraine, Svetlana and Oleg. They had been living in Vienna for many years and gave us a lot of advice on living in Austria. We exchanged phone numbers and decided to meet each other again. Svetlana offered me her help. She said I could write to her with any questions and promised to send me books to study German. I was so glad to know that there were kind people who were ready to support and help newcomers.

With high spirits and hopes for the best, we were on the way back home, listening to music in the car, when suddenly, I received a message which destroyed my mood.

'Kate, you behaved very badly. You took the things which belonged to the house and you did not clean the house. It made me sad, Bertha'.

My heart started to beat crazily. I could not believe in this nonsense. She was accusing me of taking her things and not cleaning our rooms. But it was not true. I had not taken anything of hers and I had cleaned everything.

Without hesitation, we went straight to her house to sort out this misunderstanding. I was so stressed; my hands were trembling nervously. I wanted to cry because I loved Bertha and our good relationship was very important for me.

When we arrived, Elena and her friend, Sarah, came up to me. Unfortunately, Bertha was not there.

"Elena, what happened? Why did Bertha write to me like this?" I demanded to know.

"I will tell you," said Sarah. She looked at me seriously. "You took some crockery. And now Elena can't cook."

"But I didn't. I sent Elena messages, asking her if she needed anything but she didn't reply. Have you looked everywhere?" I asked her.

"Yes, everywhere. So, give it back," she insisted.

I went into the kitchen, opened all the cupboards and showed them all the crockery. The last place which I decided to check was the place where the relevant things were kept.

They looked at me angrily.

"Is it what you need?" I asked.

"Yes, exactly," she confirmed.

"So, I am not a thief, am I?" I said.

"We did not say that you are a thief," Elena stated.

"But I can't prove to Bertha that I haven't taken anything. You should have written to me first. Bertha's opinion is very important to me. I love her," I continued.

"Okay. But why didn't you clean your rooms?" Sarah continued to interrogate me.

"I did clean them," I said. "I did my best to tidy up all our rooms and shelves in the kitchen. Elena can confirm this as she was near me while I was doing it. We were chatting all day, weren't we, Elena? Can you say something?"

"No, I was not at home all day ..." She said and looked at the floor.

After these words, I felt that I could not prove anything. I liked Elena and her daughter. I was kind to her, I thought that we were friends. I wanted to share my love with her and support her, but in the end, this was not going to be possible.

After her answer, I stopped trying to prove my innocence. My heart was broken. I returned to the car silently and we went home.

Maxim understood everything. He tried to hug me and support me.

"Kate, my dear, people can behave like this. Not all people are good," he said.

I was very frustrated. "I don't believe that a person can do such a thing. It is so unfair. I have never had such a situation in my life. I always think that all people are so kind. I need time to realise everything ..."

"Try to let it go ..." he encouraged me.

"I will. But I am not sure that it will be easy," I said.

Maxim continued, "Yes, I know how important it was for you to stay friends with Bertha. If you want, I can go and try to speak to her or her husband? Maybe, they think we have taken something else."

"Yes, that would be a good idea. I would be very glad if you did that," I answered. My eyes sparkled with joy and hope.

Maxim jumped on his bike and rushed back to Bertha's house. Martin, her husband went with Maxim to our old house and they quickly checked everything. He didn't look offended; he was open and smiled.

"Martin, do you have any claims against us?" Maxim asked him.

"Of course not," Martin answered and clapped Max on the shoulder. "Everything is okay."

Maxim came back and passed on this information.

For several weeks, I was really sad. I reflected on the reasons why people can do such things. I went to the church, talked with God, and asked the same question.

I received an answer. Actually, it was in the form of a question from God, 'Even now will you continue to say that all people are good and kind?'

This question took me by surprise. Immediately, I stopped crying and started to get all my thoughts and feelings together. I could not answer spontaneously. After some thought, I said out loud, "Yes, my God ... I believe that people inside are kind, though their actions can be wrong. And these actions were a result of their pain and wounded soul. I am forgiving Elena and Sarah. I am sure that Jesus would have done the same. Jesus met a lot of people on his way on the Earth who offended him but he continued loving them. So, I choose the same. I love them.

After saying these words, I felt such pleasant lightness in my soul. I was free from pain and obsessive questions.

"No, God, I will protect people again and again," I repeated this phrase out loud many times.

Since then, I resumed the relationship with Bertha. She sometimes wrote to me and I invited her to my parties. I really hoped that she believed me and did not feel offended. She and Martin were my Austrian angels who gave me the first help when we arrived initially.

I did not have any bad feelings about Elena. I even understood her. Her situation was much worse than mine. She was alone with a child, trying to earn money with no support. Her husband and parents were staying in Ukraine. My path could be tough but Maxim always gave me a helping hand and supported me every time during all our trials and tribulations. In Elena's situation, she was alone and lost. The war demoralised a lot of people and most of them behaved in a different way than before. I really felt this about her and wanted to wish her good luck and happiness. I made up my mind to keep only beautiful memories of her. She was a nice person and she had a right to make a mistake.

I was getting used to living in our charming new house. I had fallen in love with it at first sight.

After this situation, one very important conversation happened with my mother. She and my aunt were living in Makeevka, an area under the control of Russian military forces and they often claimed that Ukraine was destroying them and other cities. It made me very sad. My family and I were suffering a hard war. We were losing our home, life and future, but many people did not believe me. They watched Russian news and strongly believed that it was true. I wanted to call my mum to speak about it and ask her to try listening to me and understand what was going on in reality.

Despite this, the day before, I had a very strange dream. My grandmother came to me and she begged me to forgive her. She also asked me to resume my relationship with my mother. It was very important. After that she disappeared ...

I woke up and thought a lot about it. I went to the church to ask God to give me advice about this important conversation. In the evening, I was ready to call my mother and discuss everything. I was very decisive and confident, keen to correct all of our misunderstandings.

I remember the day very well and the conversation too.

"Mum, I want to tell you that I have been a witness to this bloody war. I nearly died and all this hell happened because of the Russian army. You watch the news but I saw it with my own eyes. Also, my friends, living in Kharkiv, tell me all these awful stories. If you want, I can send you real stories about the sufferings of real people.

I talked for more than twenty minutes. She listened to me attentively and at last, she said, "I promise, I will try to change my mind."

"You know without your belief, it looks like during the Second World War when a child came to her mother raped by German soldier, and her mum hugged her daughter and said, 'I love you and support you, but a German soldier is a good man. He is saving us'. Do you understand my analogy?"

"Yes, I see," she answered.

"I feel that I was betrayed by you again," I said.

"Why again?" she asked surprised.

Suddenly, all my painful feelings were building up inside of me and I asked her, "Mum, why did you leave me in childhood?"

It was a question which I had wanted to ask her all my life but one I had always been afraid to ask. I took a chance and continued, "All my life, I have been trying to find an answer to this question. You took me to granny's house when I was four. I remember exactly the moment. I was like a pet which you gave to another house. You didn't explain anything."

"I didn't want to do it, my honey ..." she said, beginning to cry. "It was a very difficult situation."

Then, she told me a story which made me shocked and frustrated, one which seemed unbelievable. It turned out that my grandmother pushed my mum to give me to her. My mother had got married very young and her husband, my father, had been drinking a lot. So, my mother used to leave me in granny's house. When I was four, my grandmother gave an ultimatum, "You must give me Kate and I will help with money, help with a home. I don't want to hear any objections." My mother was not a strong woman and agreed. Since that time, I had lived without her. They did not allow me to see my father. He had tried to see me several times but they forbade him to come closer to me.

Nobody explained to me the reasons, so I concluded that I was not good enough and that was why my mother and father had left me. I also concluded that nobody could love me. It meant that I was always trying to prove that I was good enough to be loved. This psychological trauma of the abandonment had changed my attitude to myself and to people.

All my life, I thought that my grandmother and grandfather replaced my mother and father, but this new reality revealed by my mum was changing my understanding of the situation. Now I understood why my grandmother came to my dream asking to forgive her. It looked like a true story. It was all coming together.

"Kate, before granny died, she had called me to come to her and had asked her to forgive her. She wanted to die without this sin," mum confirmed.

"Mum, what can we do now?" I asked her.

"Let's try to start again from scratch. I love you ..." she replied.

"Sorry, I cannot believe in these words. I need more time, but I will try. I promise," I said.

"And I will do all my best to make you believe," she tried to assure me. "Everyone makes mistakes, but I want to be your mum again. Give me a chance."

After this conversation, I cried for a long time. I had not expected to hear such truth. I had been thinking I was not loved by anyone, but it occurred to me that actually, everyone loved me and wanted to have me as a daughter. It was a serious discovery in my life which drastically changed everything.

When the stream of my emotions stopped, clear thoughts started coming into my mind. I was like another person. I was ready to start my life in Austria.

This knowledge freed me from pain and sufferings which I had held in my heart for many years. But then I felt light and wanted to change my life. I became more confident and ready to share my pure love with the world. Having forgiven my mother and grandmother, I became another person, happier and lighter.

When we forgive someone, especially a very close person in our life, first of all, it is important for us. It makes us free. We empty painful places in the soul and fill it up with new positive energy and happiness. Also, our life presents us miracles and generous gifts for our brave decision to forgive and let something go. It is an inevitable process of becoming happy. If we feel a lot of offences, we carry a huge load and it makes our life journey very hard and unbearable. We cannot achieve more; we cannot climb the highest peak of dreams and we cannot trust people around us. Contrast to that, without this pain we can do everything we want.

Chapter 10

Future Dreams and My Big Performance

The way to get started is to quit
talking and begin doing
— Walt Disney

After the discoveries about my childhood, I was filled with motivation and energy. I started dreaming about my future. Before that, I had been lost thinking that there were no chances for me in Austria, not knowing the language nor having any money. But suddenly, I took a notebook and wrote, 'My dreams, my goals, my plans'.

I asked myself, 'Kate, what do you want and what can you do here?' The answer came to me immediately: 'Write books and speak to people'.

The problem was that I was living in a foreign country and I could not write books in my language as I used to do earlier. Who was going to read my words here if they were written in Ukrainian? I had no chance with it. So, after a while, I made a serious decision.

On that day, on 14 April, I wrote the first page of my new book, in English.

While I was in Romania, I recorded my voice describing my journey from Kharkiv in order not to forget anything. I named the book, *The Road from Kharkiv*. It seemed the craziest idea in my life. I realised that I had no experience in writing books in English. All my books had been written in Russian and Ukrainian. Writing in English might have been a brave decision but it was certainly a risky one. It was a real challenge. I wanted to describe my experiences, write about all our challenges, pain and losses, and the real stories about the Russian-Ukrainian war. At the same time, my idea was to share my love with people, show how it was possible to find light in darkness and how I had met many kind people along the way. I didn't want my book to be just sad but inspirational as well; to give people impressions about real life and desire to search for sense, to be able to transform evil into good, dark into light and hatred into love. I was excited to have a try but, I was doubtful about my chances of success.

Every day, without stopping, I wrote two or three pages, trying to find the appropriate English words and phrases. I was writing with some trepidation. On the one hand, I considered that my book might be regarded as useless; on the other, I kept believing in its meaning. I was sure that I MUST write and present my story, my experience, my wisdom, and my love, to the world.

Once I was lying on the bed and reflecting on my approaching birthday. For many years, I had spent my birthdays organising big spiritual performances for a lot of people. About fifty people had come to my concerts where I had read my poems, including poetry written personally for those attending. I liked inspiring people and giving them a little injection of thoughts to make their lives better and happier.

I was contemplating that soon my birthday would come but I was in Austria without any possibility to read my books to people, to make them smile and happy. Suddenly, a crazy thought came to me: I would provide a performance here in Austria. I would invite Austrian people and share my love with them. I would write my inspirational poems in English and invite those who can understand English, yes, English!

This idea made me both excited and nervous. It sounded unbelievable but I was committed to do it. I would continue the tradition I had started of giving out a lot of love to as many people as possible on my birthday.

Next day, I went to see the burgermeister of the village to ask for the premises for my performance. I needed to make a first step to launch the whole process. When I told her about my idea, she was pleasantly surprised and agreed with my proposal, offering me a place for twenty people in the town hall.

The first step was done, but now I needed to write some poems. I was now thinking very optimistically. Who could organise a big performance in a foreign country without having any poems for it? I had about two months to write everything and complete all the arrangements.

Almost every day, I tried to write one poem: about God, about love, about the sense of life, about joy, happiness and desire to live with satisfaction and gratitude. I was very tired sometimes as I had lots of duties with my children, my daily work and endless routine chores at home. Nevertheless, after one month and a half, I finished with twenty pages of poems. I did it. Now, I could share God's words with the world, not just Ukraine.

In fact, I realised why God had told me in Romania that Kharkiv was not my home; that the world was my home. I saw a great mission in my stay in Podersdorf. My wings had become stronger and I was now ready to re-pay for everything I had received. I strongly believed that my responsibility was to help people where I was located wherever I found myself in the world.

It was only two weeks before my birthday. I made beautiful invitations in colour and started to give them out to different local people in the village. At first, I gave them to those who I knew already and then, I went up to the people in the streets and in the church who I had never met. It was so frightening but I was focusing on the main idea which was to present them with happiness.

Most people accepted my invitation happily and promised to come. In my list, there were already more than twenty people, so I needed a bigger place for the concert.

One day, I was asked to help my Austrian friend in the church. It was a big Christian feast and there were a lot of people in the village. I helped with the drinks and sweets. After the event, I summoned up the courage and went up to the priest, Gabriel. I asked him to help me find bigger premises for my concert. Also, I invited him personally. To my amazement, he was glad to help me and promised to come to my birthday and participate in the performance.

I was so happy. Everything was done. I had written poems, invited people and organised a place for it. Besides that, I had found a pianist and we rehearsed several times putting the music to my poems. It seemed the performance would be great. I was ready for the new challenge.

Also, I invited Bertha, and she promised to come too. I was so happy that she accepted my invitation. For two weeks, I wrote poems in English for each person who was planning to come. I tried to focus on each person, to discover their talents so that I could try to inspire and motivate them. There were thirty poems in total. Also, I printed programmes with my English poems for everyone. We ran out of cartridges for the printer. I did my best to impress everybody and to leave unforgettable memories for my Austrian neighbours and friends. I wanted to give people my love.

Soon, the day came. A lot of people arrived at the church to help me with everything: a microphone, a piano, chairs, food, and drinks. I felt support from the Austrians and of course, Maxim. A lot of people were ready to help me. They called me and offered their services. Martha cooked a big, delicious cake.

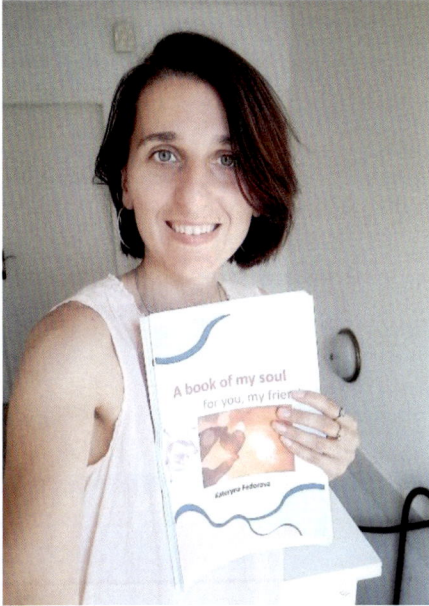

I hold the programme for my performance.

I was excited to see a lot of guests coming. Unfortunately, some people could not join us because they were ill with Coronavirus. I was a little bit upset that Bertha did not come as promised. But the concert hall was full enough. I was wearing a beautiful pink dress with elegant pink shoes. I looked light and inspirational.

I was reading my poems on the stage and Natalia, my pianist, was playing unbelievably charming music. The atmosphere was magical. The guests were listening carefully to me, picking up my wisdom and love.

I was sharing my thoughts after reading my poems. I wanted to put the idea of life in the hearts of the guests. I asked my audience lots of questions about life.

"Why do you think we are born? For what? To grow up, earn money, buy a house, a car and have a stable income to cover all expenses? No, I believe that the idea of our lives is much higher. Our soul came to get happiness on the Earth, to share sense with the world and answer necessary answers for eternal questions. It wanted to try as much as it could, to see as many places as it could and experience a great range of feelings. But most people are running, rushing somewhere non-stop. They don't notice the beauty around them. They don't do what they really want and they experience depression instead of trying to stop this senseless race to nowhere. I want people to be happier, to see millions of opportunities on the way and start living consciously."

My audience and me after my performance

At the end of the concert, I read a poem about Ukraine while Natalia played a Ukrainian hymn. Behind me, there was a video of beautiful places in Ukraine. Also, I wanted to show Austrians how my country was wonderful, and what a cruel war we were going through. The poem about Ukraine was a scream from my soul. Finally, I read the poems for each of the guests adding some kind words about their talents and skills.

After the main part of the performance, most people came up to me full of admiration and gratitude. They were full of excitement and love. My mission was complete. I was glad that all my intentions had been fulfilled.

Then, we ate cakes, drank spritzer and chatted about different things. I was looking at the people around me, and I was thinking, 'God, thank you for the opportunity to be useful to you. Look at them, they are so happy and joyful. In their eyes I see a desire to change their lives. I see that now they assess everything that they possess. You were right. My home is the world and I should spread my message around. Soon, I will speak German and will be able to give more in Austria. It takes some time. But now I have great sense, motivation to be better in order to disperse my love. You give us talents to share our love with people. With this awareness, I can move further and continue inspiring all the world. Thank you, God!'

For a long time after my concert, people wrote to me and told me that my words had really affected them. This feedback made me do more and more. This raised my confidence and motivated me.

I started to revive the jobs which I had been successfully doing in Kharkiv. I resumed doing photo sessions and giving massages. People recommended me often. Gradually, more and more new clients called me and came to use my service. At first, it was for free and then, for donation. I did not focus on money. For me, it was more important to touch them through my jobs and my skills. I tried to give them my love, my inspiration doing what I could.

In spite of my job, I kept doing charity work for Ukrainians. I went on giving psychological help for them and sent needed people some money.

My life seemed to come back to normal.

I read my poems at my performance.

Every week, I went to the church with Martha and Franz, worked on my book, studied German intensively, brought up my children and worked. I started looking ahead, not back.

Like a phoenix I was being born again. Actually, it was my second birth.

***

In 2014, the war in Donetsk had made me flee from my motherland and I tried to start my life in Kharkiv from scratch. In 2022, the situation repeated itself again. And again, I had made my decision not just to survive but to do my best to achieve my dreams and be happy again.

My life road was often rough but it did not destroy me. It made me stronger and hardy. Because of that, I felt that nothing could knock me down. I was not afraid of anything, knowing that nothing could be worse than what I had already had. I fell and stood up again and again, trying to see the sense of my trials. I went through so many life lessons and collected my life experience like something very important and valuable for humanity. I was an actor in my life and an author at the same time. I made up a plot for my life book and simultaneously, my life was a resource for itself.

My life in a foreign country could not be similar to the life in Ukraine. Nevertheless, I saw a lot of exciting and vital things which I obtained here: people, events, experience. For this short period of time, I discovered a lot about me and my life sense. I learnt to forgive people. In our life, there are always ups and downs, but in all our dark times, there is always light.

We should just make this light brighter.

Chapter 11

God Speaks to Me

*God does speak to us and we need to develop a
listening ear and recognise His voice. We need to
trust Him and take action on what we hear
— Irene Bryant, Finding Hope in
the Midst of Adversity*

It was the evening. I was lying in my bed praying to God. I was asking him about my next steps. I wanted to identify my potential possibilities and appropriate approaches to achieve my dream.

Suddenly, I felt a strange thing inside of my soul. I had a strong desire to go somewhere, to discover a new city in Austria. This thought was so weird and persistent. I could not resist it. I decided to surf the internet and search for a place I could go. I was looking through the extensive list of cities near our village, learning details about each one. I was reading about these places but I did not know or understand which one was the particular city for my future trip. I had never been on such a spontaneous journey, especially alone. In the end, I was tired and turned off my computer, finishing my search without any resolution.

It was almost midnight. Maxim and I were preparing to fall asleep. Unexpectedly, I heard a word in my soul: Graz!

I looked at my husband and confidently said, "Maxim, tomorrow I will have to go to Graz."

"Why?" he asked me, looking really astonished.

"I can't explain it to you now," I said. "I just feel that I must go to Graz and I must do it alone."

"Why Graz?" he asked.

I tried to explain. "I don't know yet but I will know later. Let me go there. I feel that it is very important. I am so afraid. It is a real challenge for me as I have never been somewhere alone and in a foreign country. But I promise to explain everything to you when I come back after the trip. I am confident that I will do that."

He checked the details about the journey to Graz and continued, "Do you know that it takes almost five hours to get there and you have to take three different modes of transport on your way?"

His words baffled me. It made me more scared. "Five hours? What am I thinking about? Should I go there and why? I could not find a logical explanation. I only felt that I must do it. Perhaps, God wanted me to do it?" I said.

"Okay, if you are sure, go. I can't resist your persistence. But please be attentive on the journey," he pleaded with me.

"Thank you, my dear. I will," I assured him.

I closed my eyes and thought, 'What am I doing? It is certainly the craziest idea I have ever had'.

In the morning, I woke up without an alarm clock. It was just after eight o'clock. Maxim said, "Kate, it is too late to go. In fifteen minutes, your bus leaves from the bus station. You won't catch it."

"Oh, no," I shouted beginning to panic and jumped quickly from the bed. I put on a dress from the wardrobe hastily, took my ID and grabbed à notebook with a pen and some sandwiches. I rushed around the house desperate to leave so I would be on time for the bus.

After ten minutes, I was running like a deer to the bus station. I couldn't breathe. I was gulping air and waving my hands to boost my running speed.

When I arrived at the station, the bus was about to leave. I jumped onto it and took a seat.

'I am on. What a crazy idea,' I thought again and sent a message to Maxim that I had made it and I was on the bus.

I sit on the train on my way to Graz.

I was going to Graz and it seemed everything was fine. It looked as if something was leading me and pushing me towards this target. I felt as if I was a leaf going with the flow, totally trusting the current.

On the train, I met a girl from Graz and she told me about the city. I asked her to recommend sightseeing locations. She gave me a detailed route for my short trip. I was on my way but thinking about my mission and the reason why I had chosen Graz.

My journey would take five hours one way and five hours back, so I would have little time to see the whole city. Could I identify the key reason for my trip? I kept asking the question to myself, 'Why am I going here? What should I find?'.

Julia was an interesting girl. She told me about her life traveling around. After her education, she decided not to go straight into the workplace but to see the world. Every month, she chose a city and went there. She found a job there too which enabled her to cover all her expenses.

While I was listening to her and her exciting travel stories, I thought about my life. I had always been doing what someone expected from me. When I used to live with my grandmother and grandfather, I did what they wanted. I liked teaching English and being a teacher, but they made me study law at university. I did not have any freedom of choice. Throughout my childhood, there was obedience and I had to follow the rules, their rules. Then I got married. I was so young, just twenty and during my marriage, I kept doing what my husband expected. There was no traveling to find new experiences. Even my second marriage repeated my previous experience. I was in the prison of endless responsibilities and duties. Because of that, I was tuning in to every word of Julia. She showed me a possible scenario of life with freedom. I didn't know what it was like, not yet anyway. I did not understand what to be free meant. Perhaps, this brave decision to go to Graz was my first step to feel this freedom.

At last, my train arrived in Graz just after midday. Julia showed me a tram stop and wished me good luck in finding what I was searching for. We hugged each other and promised to meet again.

I took a tram and went straight to the place which Julia had recommended me to see first. While I was on the tram, I saw a building and without hesitation, I pushed the stop button and got off.

I enjoy my short time in Graz.

I went across the road and approached the tall building. It was an art gallery. I was putting Julia's plan to one side but something told me to trust my inner voice. I went to the gallery and looked at all the exhibits, trying to gasp what they meant for me, what emotions they triggered. I was wondering why I had stopped exactly here.

Many times, I had thought that I wanted to paint too, to express vivid pictures from my mind. It could also help me to give my love to people through pictures.

When I finished with the gallery, I went outside. My trip was a constant conversation with my soul, so again, I asked it where it wanted to go next. All the time in Graz, I felt that I had been there before. Everything was so familiar. I did not use a navigator nor maps. It sounds a bit strange but I knew this city very well. I was walking around like I had been living there all my life. I felt deja vu all the time.

In the distance, I saw an old church and decided to go in. Inside, I had so many overwhelming feelings. I prayed and cried while talking to God. I felt happy being there. It was a moment of truth.

When I was leaving the church, I noticed a photo of a woman on the wall and some words at the bottom of the picture, 'When the shadow of fear disappears, you will get true happiness and joy'. I took a photo of this portrait and went out.

After the church, I spent about three hours in the city, visited two more churches, historical places and ate pizza in a restaurant. I was pleasantly surprised that I could speak German. Maybe, this city provoked me to speak it? There, I was so happy and did not want to go back.

Later, I returned to the railway station in order to go home. I easily found my train and took a seat near the window. I closed my eyes and felt real satisfaction and excitement after the trip. But my question, 'Why did I come here?' had not been answered. It made me a bit sad.

While I was going back, I met another Austrian girl and we discussed the meaning of life. I really wanted to inspire her to make some changes in her life.

Her name was Laura and she told me, "I am a manager in a bank but I do not like my job. Maybe, at some point I will try something else."

"But what do you like?" I asked.

"I like writing. I wanted to be a journalist," she said.

"But why are you doing what is not your passion? I asked her.

"Because it is stable and provides money," she replied.

"Sorry, but does this stable life give you happiness?" I asked.

"I'm not sure. I feel bored every day at work," she confirmed.

"If you could do your favourite job, what would you feel? I inquired.

"I would be full of positivity and bright emotions. It would give me a lot of energy," she said.

"What would you have to do to get this job as a journalist?" I asked again.

"I suppose I should get an education and find a good vacancy," she replied.

"You know when people do the job they like, they certainly do more for other people as well as satisfying themselves more. Take a risk and follow your dream. Don't get side-tracked. Just listen to your inner soul and soon, you will obtain your awaited happiness," I said.

"You are right. I am young enough and can try harder in order to get an education, change my job and achieve a goal," she agreed.

"Yes. Why not? The main important life goal is to be happy. And only WE can create the conditions for our happiness," I assured her.

We were talking all the way about her possible future, sometimes recalling some painful topics about the war in

Ukraine. In the end, we exchanged contacts and said goodbye, but promised to share good news with each other.

Late in the evening, I arrived home. I was really exhausted but excited. I was full of pleasant feelings and memories.

Maxim asked me, "Have you understood the reason for going to Graz?"

"I am not sure that I got it," I told him. "It was an amazing trip but I don't feel the exact answer yet. I might need more time."

"I told you before that it was a crazy idea. But now I will go alone to Vienna next week and you will stay with the children. That's fair," he said.

"Okay, deal," I said.

Next day, I uploaded some photos on Facebook and described my magical trip. Suddenly, I got a private message from an unknown woman. 'The woman in the photo from the church in Graz is very similar to you. It is very interesting to explore', it read.

After her message, I looked at the photo attentively and I was stunned. She really was my double.

Soon, I received again a message from the same woman, 'Kate, I've read about this woman in the photo. Her name is Therese of Lisieux. And I suppose you are very similar. She seemed to have the same life mission as you. Maybe, for you, it sounds very strange but I am pretty sure about it. She resembles you not only by appearance. Read about her and you will understand everything.'

I began to find out about Therese and her life. The more I read about her, the more I was convinced that the woman could be right.

She was an amazing person. She was born in a very religious family. When Therese was four, her mother died and her father brought her up with her four sisters. Therese had a very special relationship with God. She was a very kind child with an open heart and wanted to love the whole world. I also grew up without my mother from when I was four. I perceived the world as she did: I called God 'my daddy' and spoke to him almost every day. Since my early days, I had believed that I could change the world. I helped everyone with love: animals, people, kids.

Therese of Lisieux

Theresa became a nun at a very early age, when she was only fifteen. She wanted to serve just God. She had to make a lot of compromises to be allowed to join the monastery. When I was a teenager, I also dreamt of being a nun and waited for my eighteenth birthday to try. But I changed my mind and wanted to be useful and helpful among people in a different way.

The period in the Carmelite's monastery was very hard for her. The nuns behaved rudely to her, but she managed to develop absolute love for them. She reflected a lot on the topic of love. She was eager to share her view of love with the whole world.

Therese was more than ever determined to do something great for God and for others. She thought of herself as a new Joan of Arc, dedicated to the rescue not only of France but of the whole world. She always stated, 'I was born for glory'. She perceived her life's mission as one of salvation for all people. She was to accomplish this by becoming a saint. She understood that her glory would be hidden from the eyes of others until God wished to reveal it.

Freed from herself, she embarked on her 'Giant's Race'. She was consumed, like Jesus, with a thirst for souls. 'My heart was filled with charity. I forgot myself to please others and, in doing so, became happy myself'.

Therese wanted to stay humble, while trusting God and his will. She developed her other qualities such as the ability to love and accept everything that God gave. 'It is impossible for me to grow up, so I must bear with myself such as I am with all my imperfections. But I want to seek out some means of going to heaven by a little way that is very straight, very short and totally new'.

When she died at the age of twenty-four, she believed that her life was really just beginning for God, promising to spend her time in heaven doing good on earth. She promised an internal 'shower of Roses'.

My life has changed dramatically since I found out about Therese. I spent much time reflecting on our resemblance. I tried solving the mystery which God had presented to me. Why did he do that? Why did he ask me to go to Graz? And why did I find out about Therese?

All my life, I had been praying to God to give me an answer. 'Who am I? What is my sense?'. And now, he gave me that but I was unaware what to do with this treasure.

I made a decision: to finish Therese's mission, to give people love, to help them in their earthly life and direct them to God's road. Step by step, I opened new sides of my personality, my soul which I became very close to. And certainly, I was very close to God. He seemed to speak to me every time. He wanted me to do what Therese could not. She died at a very early age. And during my life, I was in a hurry to live. I was greedy to obtain everything in the world. I was eager to try everything, to help everyone, to love the world. However, I felt that I had little time, not enough to complete everything.

Perhaps, because of that, I managed to get two degrees: Law and English philology. Also, I had education as a psychologist, photographer, and masseur. Besides that, since my childhood, I had been volunteering nonstop. I helped people with different diseases, orphans, disabled children, homeless and children dying from cancer. When I lived in Kharkiv, I used to go to them every week for many years. I couldn't stop providing this help. I always said, 'Who can do this if not me?'. I have never had any pity for them, just love. For me, all these poor and ill people were like everyone else. Also, I felt that they were particularly sincere and open.

I strongly believe that before coming to Earth, our souls choose a lot of different trials and obstacles on their way. The more difficult their life, the more important tasks their souls have to accomplish. If a person has a very hard childhood or serious illness, their soul is very old and knows exactly what it should get from it. I do not feel pity for these people, I admire, support and love them.

This discovery about Therese motivated me to do more about realising my life mission. I constantly added to my book, page by page, adding my soul to it and sharing my thoughts with my future readers. Certainly, I could not be like Therese, but I could develop myself and evolve my soul more in order to fulfil it with more bliss and kindness. If I was lighter and inspired, I could contribute more into the world. Therese became my lighthouse which directed me to my shore.

Chapter 12

A Trip Home

Life Taught me Love is Risky.
Death taught me to love even more
— Maxime Lagace

In November 2022, I made a decision to visit Kharkiv. The reason for my journey was to deal with issues concerning our language school. The landlords of the school had sent us regular payment demands. We knew that we were not able to cover all our expenses and I did not see any other option than the closure of the school completely, although this decision was extremely hard for me. The plan was for me to go to Kharkiv alone while Maxim looked after the children in Austria. I would try to resolve everything and then return.

I pretended to be calm and confident with all of this. I acted as if I was ready to go and that everything would be okay. But the reality was that I was very scared. My heart was telling me not to go. I had many dark thoughts which made me fed up and listless.

In spite of all my worries, I trusted in God. I decided to deal with all these matters positively, especially as this could help me move on and to start my new life. In addition, of course, it would be my opportunity to see Ukraine, my lovely city of Kharkiv and our flat, where we had been living happily before the war began.

Before the trip, I tried to find people who could help me with my school, especially those who wanted to buy or take away the furniture. I did my best to do some preparatory work, but nobody reacted to my messages. So, I was about to buy tickets and ready to set out, when at the last minute, my friend Tanja said that her husband could help me with the furniture. He had time at weekends. Then, my friend Jana also informed me that her ex-husband was going through Vienna to Kharkiv. I wrote to him immediately and asked him to pick me up. I offered to pay part of the petrol. Suddenly, my journey was coming together, step by step.

In the last few days before the journey, I was very nervous. My family supported me, as did my friends, Martha and Franz, who were extremely worried about me. They understood the risk which I would be taking and tried to help me as much as they could. I remember exactly the moment when Martha presented me with a pair of her shoes to keep me warm in Ukraine, gave me her medallion of Saint Maria and a holy small icon. She read a prayer and she blessed me for the journey. She asked me to write to them to tell me about my activities there. After that, I went to the church and asked God to be next to me all the time on my trip and help me to come back safe and sound to my children. I wanted to finish everything and come back to the people who loved me and would always be there waiting for me.

The next day, I went to Vienna to meet with Yury who was going to take me to Kharkiv. The weather was sunny and warm. It looked like everything was supporting me and wanted me to stay calm and happy. While Maxim was driving, at that moment, I felt that everything would be okay. I was ready to go. I was heading straight to my country, my city, my flat. I was looking forward to seeing my native landscapes, to breathe my country's air and to see Ukrainians walking in the streets.

In Vienna, I said goodbye to Maxim. I hugged and kissed him and promised to come back as soon as possible.

Then, I jumped quickly into Yury's car. While I was there, many thoughts came into my mind. I was overwhelmed by so many different feelings and emotions. Yury was not so talkative, so we were silent most of the time, deep into our own thoughts. I was thinking about my meeting and seeing my city and my flat. I was wondering what I would feel and what reaction I would have when I arrived. I also thought about my school, trying to plan out my future steps and organising in my mind what I had to do there. The most frightening moment was the negotiation with the landlords. They owed sixty thousand hryvnas (approximately $1,600) and asked us to pay about ten thousand hryvnas (approximately $270) for heating. I was so afraid of this negotiation as I was not sure that I could prove anything legally at war time. The landlords were rich people and they would hardly make concessions.

By nightfall, we were already in Ukraine. Crossing the border was not so difficult. We were very tired and wanted to have a rest. We tried to find a hotel room. I called many places but everything was booked up. Yury was busy driving, trying to concentrate on the road and staying awake when suddenly, we saw a little hotel. Fortunately, they had two rooms available. We sighed in relief. I went into my room and sat down on the sofa. I was looking around and thinking about how I was back in Ukraine. I took a shower and hid under a lot of blankets. The room was freezing. It took me some time to get used to the idea that I was not in Austria anymore. I was thinking about my family and also, my future plans. The thoughts were distracting me from sleep, but at last, my brain gave up and I fell into my dreams.

All night, I had nightmares about how I was running away from the tanks and how Maxim was dying. I woke up several times trembling from fear and from extreme cold.

In the morning, I opened my eyes and felt that I was totally frozen. There was no electricity, no heating and the water had stopped. At that moment, I thought again, 'I am in Ukraine, in a warring country …' These sad thoughts were replaced by the beautiful snowy view from my window. The trees were covered by a thin layer of white snow. It looked like I was in a fairy-tale. There were magic landscapes with morning sparking rays falling softly on the tree branches. Although it was cold inside, I opened the window, stretched my arms and closed my eyes to experience the moment. While I was filling up with the energy of the Ukrainian sun and snow, suddenly I got a message from Yury, 'Go!'.

The snowy view that started our second day.

The second part of our journey was like the first. For most of it, we were silent. We wanted to arrive as soon as possible, so we kept looking at the satnav directing us to our destination.

At the end of the journey with Yury, we discussed one important topic. He was furious having heard about my decision to give up and pay money to the landlords. He tried to convince me to fight more and keep this money. His argument was that I could use the money for my children.

"Business doesn't like kindness. It is a cruel world and being kind means being stupid in business," he said.

After our discussion, I was determined to prove my position and not to pay for heating, proving that this money could be taken from their funds. Yury's words got stuck in my mind, "It is your karmic task which you must solve in a way that lasts," he had said.

When we approached Kharkiv, I saw broken houses, destroyed buildings, burnt cars and trains. These pictures made me sad. Tears were falling from my eyes nonstop. My country, what have they done with you? How did they dare? I wanted to close my eyes so that I wouldn't have to see these views through my window. It was unbearably difficult to accept what was happening to my country.

But I summoned up some courage and forced myself to look bravely at the destruction caused by the Russian invasion. I wanted to take some photos to show my Austrian friends and other foreigners, who were unaware what hell Ukrainians were going through. Inside of me, there was such an unspeakable frustration and anger. I wanted to shout out to the world and beg them to help us, to finish people's sufferings. Ukrainians were going to work every day not knowing if they would come back alive. They would go to the shop and it could be for the last time. They would go to bed not knowing if they would wake up. They were living in stress and fear and nobody knew when it would finish.

The last few kilometres were very difficult. They seemed never-ending. I was looking forward to going home.

Late at night, my dream had come true. I was standing near my house with two small bags: one was with my clothes and another full of things for Ukrainians who might need something. I knew that my little bag was not comparable with tons of clothes from big charity organisations. But I could not come empty-handed. I wanted to help as much as I could.

I opened the porch door and went upstairs to the ninth floor. It was dark and silent inside. I used my telephone to light the way. At last, out of breath and with pain in my hands from the bags, I approached my flat's door. With trembling hands, I opened it and went in.

I stepped inside, looked around and slowly kneeled on the floor, holding the bags in my hands tightly. Something started to choke me in my chest. I made an effort and stood up, took off my coat, scarf and gloves and came into the living room. Then, I gave in and burst into tears. I started crying heavily. It was not simple crying. I sobbed, whimpered and moaned like a wolf. I could not control myself. These feelings had been kept deep inside of me for many months and I had not allowed myself to let them out. But that night, I was alone: no children to take care of, no husband to obey, no people to help. I was just with myself in the silent room of my past. My tears were flowing nonstop. I could not help crying. All my pain pent up across nine-months broke out. I was like a little girl, sitting in the corner in the living room and kissing the floor where my kids had played. I kissed Tishka's bed. I crawled from one room to another one and cried louder and shriller. I looked at any objects in the rooms and I saw a movie of my happy past life. And it was killing me. I was angry at the war, the Russians and everyone who had stolen my happy life there. I wanted to stop the movies and closed my eyes tight covering them with my hands. My energy was running low. For what seemed like hours, I kept crying and nothing and no-one could help me to stop it.

At last, I took some soothing medicine and tried to calm down. I sat on the bed and stared at the wall. I was sitting in this position for half an hour calmly, not moving. I was looking at the bare wall in order not to see the movies in my mind.

Accidentally, something fell on the floor and I looked at it. This triggered the second stage of my hysterics. I saw another movie. On the floor near the bed was where I had been sitting on 24 February hiding from the bombs. I remembered everything so clearly. In the flat, everything was in the same place as it was on that day. I went through that day again and again until I collapsed on the bed and fell asleep. It was almost five o'clock in the morning.

The next day, I woke up and went to the kitchen to find some food. I had not eaten anything for some time. Obviously, our fridge was empty. We had allowed our neighbour to take everything. I was so weak and needed some energy. I went into my bedroom again, found my best, beautiful clothes, put them on and went out. I wanted to eat in the cafe where I had been going with Maxim before the war. It was our cafe, our secret and romantic place.

The weather was bad. There was a harsh wind and showers. The ground was wet and very slippery. I kept walking, determined to reach the cafe. I ordered a sandwich with fruit tea, I found the same place where we used to sit. I looked good with a beige coat, red dress, red beret and long, red earrings. I wanted to look elegant and luxurious in my city. I wanted to be the same person who I had been before the war.

I ate the sandwich trying to control my emotions. Suddenly, I heard the song *You are beautiful* by James Blunt and it was a trigger for me. Again, I started to cry. It was a grey view through the windows and it was raining so heavily. I cried as I remembered my happy days in this place.

Back in our flat. I struggle with the memories.

I managed to get myself together and stood up. I fought these attacks of pain every time. I did not want to surrender. I decided to go to the beauty salon which I used to use before the war. I went there to be among people. I felt that I needed support. They corrected my brows and did a manicure. I was sitting and listening to them, trying to answer their questions.

My face was red and swollen from all the tears. Inside of me, there was a continuous battle with despair.

I was preparing for the next challenge: the closure of my school. Habib, Tanja's husband, promised to help with it. So, after all the beauty procedures, I went to him.

We entered the school and my heart squeezed again from pain.

'No crying, please', I said strictly to myself.

I gulped all my pain and with a cold face started to prepare everything. I wrote everywhere on social networks about closing my school and asked people to come and take what they needed. Some furniture, I planned to sell, some, to give away, some to use as gifts. All the papers, books, and stationery were going to be given away. I acted bravely and calmly. Habib took apart the furniture and I emptied the shelves, chests and bookcases. Some people came and took some things. My six rooms there were becoming emptier and emptier. One woman called me and said that she was from a charity organization which helped people during the war. They needed a lot of furniture. Of course, I gave a lot of desks, bookcases and chairs to her. Also, she agreed to help me to take the rest of the furniture into my garage the next day. I was happy to see how good deeds turned into other good deeds. In the evening, we were tired as we had done a big part of the job. My friend Irina came to see me and helped to take some computer devices to my flat in her car.

After that, we went to a cafe and had a talk. She told me the sad story of her evacuation and how many tragedies she had been through. I was listening to her and realised how much pain this war brought for people. Then we brought up a topic about the purpose of life.

"Kate, I wanted to do a lot of things in my life but every time something distracted me, some obstacles got in my way. Now, it is a war; last year it was Coronavirus," she said.

"Irina, there is never an excellent time to realise our purpose in life. There is always something in our way. Our souls knew about it when they were going onto the Earth. Our task is to learn how to manage with these difficulties and overcome fears and lack of confidence, but at the same time, we must keep going with our main life mission. In this storm of events and tragedies, we must do what we must do," I replied.

"I understand but how it is possible to do anything in the warring city under attack from bombing and without decent conditions for work?" she asked.

"You are here because you made a decision to be here and it means it is a perfect place for realising your purpose. Time during the war has an advantage: we have nothing to lose. We can try to do anything and start new professions, try our hand in different spheres. We must find how to survive: physically and mentally. In Austria, I have tried new things also, adjusting to new conditions. Have you ever thought, maybe this war is a necessary trigger to push us to important actions, an impulse to launch what we wanted to do but we were afraid to take the first step? It is a time to see what we are really capable of," I explained.

"I see what you mean," she said. "You are right. Now, I am excited by the process of packaging new products. I like to control all the processes, organise all the details. I like the moment when a new product is being born. It is a wonderful process, the birth of a new star. I want to do something important in the world and for people. I am searching for my purpose and trying to find new clues on how to realise my life mission," she said.

"It sounds good," I said. "I am sure that your life is valuable. God helps people through us. We are his helpers for making good deeds. And it is very important to be generous to let God give his love with our hands, with our words and with our actions. You are here and it means that your place of realisation is here. The sky will do everything to save your life as he needs you," I concluded.

"Oh, yes. I want to tell you that I have had so many times when I could have died. My death was so close to me but miracles happened and I stayed alive. I can't explain how it was but I saw this magic," she outlined.

"Irina, ask yourself the questions several times: 'Why does God save my life? For what greater reason?' When you get the answer in your soul, you became calmer and happier. You could see your destination and keep going forwards. I believe in you," I assured her.

"Thank you, my dear Kate," she said. "Even in such hard times, you find power and vital words for supporting people."

After dinner, we parted. I went to buy some food for the next day and she drove home. After the trials at my school, I headed back to my next room of torture, my flat.

When I entered, again, a cloud of depression fell over me. But I tried to resist it. I found a little alcohol in the fridge, drank it and went straight into the living room. I had a strong desire to throw away a lot of things from the shelves. So, that second night, I spent my time sorting out the papers in the bookcases and packing enormous bags with rubbish. I wanted to free my space from pain. In the early morning, I went to bed.

The next day was much more difficult than the first two. When I arrived at the school, a lot of people were waiting for me. They wanted to take things. They had responded to my announcement. I gave them what they wanted and I carried on packing boxes.

Soon, more and more people came to take stationery, games for children, books, and furniture. At the same time, there were more than twenty people searching for things that could be useful to them. Frequently, I was being asked, "Can I take this?"

"Yes, you can …" I answered sadly, every time.

I allowed them to take simple papers or cards. But all of these things were like a part of me. I felt as if they were skinning me alive. Each book, each pack of English cards, a set of games and other bits and pieces had all been collected by me over twelve years. They were my treasure, my achievement, my victory. And then, I had to give them all away. At least that made better sense than just throwing them in the rubbish bin. At least, I was giving a second life to the possessions from my school. 'It would be fair and kind', I thought as I helped them to pack their items.

My employee came to take her possessions too. She was a teacher in my school who had been working for me for six years. She took the bags which I had prepared for her in advance and came up to me. My heart wanted to cry.

"Sofia, thank you for everything," I said to her. "You did a good job. I value everything that you have done for me and our school. I remembered the day you came to me. You were so young and unconfident. But now you are so cool."

"You believed in me, you created me from scratch. I am a teacher just because of you and your belief and support," she replied.

"You were always like a daughter to me," I assured her.

"Yes, I know. You were like a mum to me too. I hope the war is over and we will revive our school. You have invested so much in it: money, soul, days, hard work, love. It is so painful to see how people are taking everything," she said. I could not disagree with her.

"I know, my dear. I believe in you. I want you to go further. You are incredible. I love you so much." I said these words and started crying.

I was holding her arms in front of my chest and kissing them intensively. I did not want to say goodbye to her, I wanted to stop everything and return to our peaceful, happy, working days in the school.

At last, after I hugged her tightly one more time, she left. Tears were falling from my eyes as she disappeared in the distance. Still, people in the room kept asking me, "Can I take this?"

More and more people were coming into the school and leaving with full bags. Also, one woman came to take everything from my massage cabinet which I had organised for my practice before the war. I gave her everything so that she could organise her own massage business.

Later, one more girl came to the school. She greeted me and said, "I've heard you are giving away things from your English school. My dream was to open my own school for children. When I saw your announcement, I decided to come."

"Yes, you must realise your dreams. I will help you. You can do whatever you want here," I told her.

She spent a lot of time choosing the necessary things for her future English school. I gave her some advice and suggestions. In the end, she had four heavy bags with everything as well as two white boards.

"Kate," she concluded, "I am ready. I have everything for opening my own school. I have no words. You have done so much for me. I don't know how to thank you. I hope that I will have such an opportunity. I am grateful to you from the bottom of my heart. I understand how much work and love went into it. I know that all these things will make many little hearts happy, I promise to send photos of happy children's faces. Let your goodness return to you as a resource and magical helper at the right moment."

"I am happy to know that my twelve years of hard work will be a help for opening a new school. I will give you my star of success. I believe in you," I replied.

She left and I stayed in the middle of the mess with sad eyes but joy amongst the people who were becoming happy as a result of my gifts. For me, it was an end, while for many of these people, it was a beginning of something new.

'I must be strong and generous', I thought and kept going with the task.

After many hours of intensive work, we were left with near empty rooms. We put the rest of the furniture in the hall to take to our garage. There were a lot of big conference tables, desks, a heavy sofa, a lot of chairs and other items. It looked as if we were moving a really big school. Soon, some men from the charity organization came and helped us to put all the furniture into their van.

When we closed the school and went towards the garage, our real adventure began. We had not expected the problems we were about to face. The van arrived at a certain place and Maxim called and explained to them the location of our garage. It was a special garage corporation, which consisted of hundreds of garages with very low ceilings for cars.

The driver said, "We can't go inside. The ceilings are too low for us. So, we will leave the furniture here and you will do it by yourself. Also, we are in a hurry and we should go soon."

They unloaded their van and put all the furniture outside. Suddenly, we realised that they had offloaded everything in the wrong place. Our garage was at the other end of the site. We were in panic and despair about what we would do. They unloaded everything for us but then they left, although not before helping Habib with one of the heaviest tables.

We were there alone in darkness with a long line of heavy furniture under the snow, in cold weather and with no hope or idea of what to do. I wrote a begging post on Facebook, asking someone to help us.

While we were waiting for help, I found a metal wheelbarrow buried under the snow and started to carry the furniture from the place where the men unloaded it to the entrance of our garage. It took me fifteen minutes to do one ride. Habib put the heaviest tables on his back and carried them to the garage. We were cold and exhausted. We spent a lot of time loading and carrying but it did not look like there was any progress.

Then, my friend Andrew arrived. He had a jeep, so he offered to move the furniture in his car a bit at a time. Finally, we completed the task. It took us five trips. I could not feel my fingers and wanted to collapse.

Andrew was our angel. He really saved us from a catastrophe. I thanked him and Habib. These men were my heroes that day. When we parted near the school, I closed everything and went to the restaurant to eat. I had not eaten since the morning. I was hardly walking. I visited the restaurant where I had had my great performances and where hundreds of guests had come to see and hear my poems. This place was the runway of my success. I sat in the corner, eating my dinner in loneliness and with tears, remembering the old, happy days.

The wheelbarrow I found for moving the furniture.

In the late evening, I came home. I cleaned the house until dawn. When I had no more energy left, I fell down exhausted on the bed in my clothes. I slept badly, waking up frequently from nightmares. The nights in Kharkiv were turning out to be a real challenge for me.

In the morning, I had an unexpected message from the woman called Oksana who had come to the school earlier. She invited me to come to her and she would give me a massage and apply some soothing techniques.

"Kate, you gave me your massage table from the school and I wanted to do something for you. My dream to be a masseur can come true. It is because of you," she said.

"Yes, I will come to you. Give me your address." I answered. I needed a break and support. My offer to her was being returned to me.

Oksana appeared in my life spontaneously a few years before. I had just started my career as a photographer. She came to one of my photo sessions and since that time, we had known each other. I always inspired her to do what she dreamed about. She also took my coaching sessions, came to my performances and bought my books. When I studied at massage courses, she wanted to try her hand in it and studied at the same school. Now, I had given her my massage table which could give her a chance to realise her purpose in life.

I came to her house which was on the other side of the city but I felt that I had to go. It was important for both of us.

She gave me some food and did the relaxation procedures.

Next, I managed to call my landlord to discuss the question about the money and to arrange a meeting. She was against my proposal and said, "Why should I help you? Who can help me? I have so many problems with my cottages and my son. Let's meet tomorrow at half past eight and finish this conversation."

I hung up and, suddenly, I felt pity for this woman. I realised that I was really a rich person, as I had everything: loving children and a husband, supportive friends and parents. I did not want to argue with her, I just wanted to return to my family as soon as possible.

Oksana gave me a cup of tea with pancakes and admitted to me, "Kate, thank you for the massage table but I am so afraid of announcing myself and my services. I am afraid of people's reaction."

Oksana helps me relax using my old massage table.

"My dear, I am completely confident that we must realise our mission every time. We have a responsibility to do God's job. It's our holy duty. Do you know how God helps people?" I asked her.

"When we pray, he helps us somehow," she replied.

"Yes, but how?" I asked again.

"I don't know. Maybe, he sends us something," she said.

"God can help us just with someone's hands, other people's hands. I will try to give one example. Imagine a girl. Her name may be Anna. She prays and asks God to help her. She really needs help and cries and begs for a sign from somewhere. God listens to her and looks for someone who could help her and send her his words and his love. He looks for someone who obtains certain qualities and resources which are necessary to convey his message to Anna. He finds you, for example, and believes that you can do that for him. He sees that you can do that through your massage or other services. He sends you the thoughts, putting them into your packet of dreams and starts waiting. He waits and waits until you make the first steps. Soon Anna comes and gets her message from God.

"Now you see, how it is important to realise your life purpose and do what you should do. Your hands and your words are his hands and words. It is not important at all what other people will say about you. Your focus must be on this girl. You are helping people every time. You should forget about your ego and do your service bravely. I believe in you," I said finishing my words.

"Thank you, Kate. You are right. I promise to be braver and talk about my services every time," she confirmed.

"And send me one hundred photos with one hundred of your clients," I requested of her.

"Yes, I will," she answered and laughed.

I thanked her for her support and went home. I had to do a lot of cleaning in my flat.

While I was cleaning and packing new rubbish sacks, a man called Sergey came. He brought me a second key from the school. I invited him in for tea. He looked very miserable and wanted to speak to me. It transpired that he had broken up with his girlfriend and needed some advice.

"Kate, what can I do? I realised that I love her but she does not love me back. I am desperate. Everything reminds me of her in the flat," he said.

"How long did you live together?" I asked.

"Just two months … And after that, the war started. She went to England and I stayed here. I made so many mistakes, I understand that now," he confirmed, looking sad.

"Tell me what you actually did," I asked him.

"We had some disagreements about cleaning in the house, with money and a future marriage. We wanted different things and neither of us would make concessions," he confirmed.

"I see what you mean," I said. "Actually, I was in my first marriage for eight years and in the second, for about ten. So, I have had experience of such stages in relationships. At first, you must understand what is important for you: being happy with a person or being true. Answer the questions, 'Are you ready to be better for the person? Do you really love her? What do you want to feel in the end?' If you see positive answers and you feel as if you want to fight for your love, you must do whatever you have to in order to be happy and make your partner happy. Love is not only butterflies in the stomach, but also always about the hard work needed for improvements, overcoming difficulties and becoming better and better in the loving union.

"In my relationships, I also made so many mistakes. I was stubborn and wanted my way to prevail, but there's always a solution for any problem. We can always find a perfect alternative for any difficult situation. We must go beyond the current problem and seek out these potential solutions. For example, my husband liked order and cleanliness in the flat, but I could not satisfy his expectations. We had so many quarrels about it. Then, we decided to solve it. He lowered his expectations a little bit and I raised my focus on cleaning and order. We found a golden balance. It is a simple example of how to make a relationship better.

"Many people give up and they don't want to see the other options. They want to have just what they want and they lose the opportunity to be happy and loved. But who said that to love is easy? When we transfer into the love stage, we always have trials. They are like exams which we must pass to progress. If we fail, we have to pass it with another person again and again. If you really want to love and be loved, you must be flexible, wise and persistent in order to make your common life happier.

"I love my husband so much because I always remember how many difficulties we managed to overcome, how many problems we managed to solve and how many other trials I am ready to go through with him further, only with him."

"Oh, now I want to write to her and say everything, about my feelings and my readiness to struggle for our love," he said enthusiastically. "Thank you, Kate."

When Sergey left, I went to bed. I did not have the energy for anything else.

In the morning, I had the important meeting with the landlord of the school. I woke up with such a warm feeling in my heart. I felt love for this woman. I took my written book *Start Living!* and wrote a postcard for her. I wanted to present it to her to support her and give my love.

When I went out, I went to her with excitement and happiness. I did not understand what had happened to me at night, but I was full of positive emotions, and my spirits were flying high. I asked myself, 'Kate, what do you have in your arsenal for these negotiations?' And I got an answer, 'Love! I am going with love'.

I met her and I saw a business lady in a mink coat with a strict appearance and serious voice. She was talking about money, walls and heating. But I was waiting until I could give her my book and say good, supportive words. When, eventually, she finished and we signed all the documents, I said, "Valeria, I have a present for you," and I gave her my book. "I hope it can support you in dark times and make you smile."

She read my postcard inside of the book and looked at me with tenderness. At that moment, she was another person, sincere and open, with sad and lonely eyes.

"Thank you, Kate. This is so unexpected. I'm impressed. It is so hard now for me. The Russians destroyed my house, my son lost his job, and my husband died. Thank you for this book and your sympathy," she said.

I hugged her with love and left the office.

In the distance, I saw as she opened the doors of her jeep for an elderly couple who were supposed to ask her for help. I was standing nearby, looking at her kind deeds and thanking God for this. I chose the right decision; I was happy to see how my action changed this woman. Maybe, it was the first time when a person had behaved like this for her, with love and support instead of aggression and anger. She became a little bit happier and kinder and it cheered my soul.

When I came home, the electricity was off. There was no heating, no water, no signal, no internet. Sirens were sounding outside and I was alone in my flat. It was so frightening. I did not know what was going on, I could not read any news or call anyone.

When it was dark, I took my oil paints, a canvas and started painting a picture. There were candles around me and I was deep in the process of painting. I wanted to transform my fear and pain into art. For several hours, I painted a picture of flowers. I called it, *A Bucket of Victory*. When I finished it, I packed my bags for my homeward journey and went to bed. The next day was my final day. Soon, I would be with my family. I was looking forward to seeing them all.

I was concerned that my family might be worried about me as I was offline. During that time, they wrote to me often. I was even surprised to know that they loved me so much and cared about me a lot. I was so happy to get a message from Misha, 'Mum, how are you?' he asked. Annya also sent me a message, 'Mummy, how did you sleep? I love you', and there were many messages from Maxim. He asked me how I was doing and expressed his support and love. I found myself asking, 'Where's my home? Here or in Austria? A lot of people are waiting for me: my children, my husband, my friend Tanja, Martha and Franz, Jacqueline. Tomorrow, I am going to them and my life will be back to normal again'.

My painting, *A Bucket of Victory*

My last day in Kharkiv started at seven o'clock in the morning. I woke up and established that there was not any progress with electricity or the internet. Finally, I completed a last clean of the flat and prepared to go to the railway station, packing my bags and checking everything. While I was sorting out my possessions, I found a bag with an envelope with five thousand hryvnas (approximately $140). It was exactly the same sum of money, which I needed for my journey back. It looked like a miracle. Yesterday, I chose love not money and God gave me this help. He took care of me. It meant that I had made a correct decision and I received an award from the sky.

I prepare to say goodbye to our flat in Kharkiv.

I said goodbye to my flat and set out. It was a long way back home. When I arrived at the railway station, I found out that all the trains were delayed, including mine. The train should have arrived at one o'clock in the afternoon, but a woman in the information office said it would be there in seven hours. It sounded unbelievably horrible. I wondered what I could do. I must go by bus to Vienna tomorrow. If I didn't arrive on time in Ujgorod, I would not be able to go to my family and lose a lot of money as I had paid for a ticket. What could I do in Ujgorod? I had a stream of questions in my mind and no answers. I decided to stay at the railway station and wait for a miracle. I ate cold pancakes and sat on my bags on the floor in the corner of the hall. Soon, I was cold, my telephone had low battery and I felt miserable. I was sitting and hoping that God would help me.

Those seven hours seemed to last so long. It was like eternity. I was in the railway station so long that I had time to make new friends there and do a lot of things before leaving. At last, at eight o'clock in the evening, my train arrived and I ran to the platform. I took my place and sighed, 'I'm in', I thought, 'Now, I should solve my next task with the bus to Vienna'.

I was very tired, so I ate some food and went to sleep. 'Morning is wiser than evening', I thought and fell asleep.

In the morning, my neighbour from the compartment announced to me excitedly. He knew my problem with the bus, "Kate, you won't believe it, but the train has been going so fast all night and almost managed to catch up with the fixed timetable. Maybe, you can get your bus."

"It would be great," I said.

I was full of hope and sent a message to Maxim. Everything was going on for me. I started to be positive again.

The train was really dashing to its destination, making very short stops at the stations. I had a chance to be on time.

When I had just four stations to go, I started panicking. I went to the train conductor to ask for advice. He said that I must get off the train now and run to the bus station and take a taxi. This way, I would be able to take a bus on time. By train, it was impossible.

I came back to my compartment and I saw a poor man, who accidentally sat in front of me waiting for his stop. I found out from him that he was a widow and he was going to his three children. I gave him some sweets and shared my situation. He answered calmly, "Don't jump from the train. God is taking care of you. Trust him."

But I was thinking about my children and the risk of missing my bus.

"I must go. Can you help me with my bedclothes? I must pack up my things and run," I said.

'Yes, of course, I will," he said.

I did not know this man, but at that moment, he was like my best friend. He helped me with my bedclothes and my bags. At our parting, he said, "God blesses you. Don't be afraid. He is behind you."

"What is your name?" I asked him.

"My name is Ivan," he answered and disappeared into the crowds.

Sometimes, I think that this man was just a figment of my imagination. Later, I would remember his words often.

I jumped from the train and ran very quickly across the rails to the bus station. I took the first taxi even though he proposed a very high price for the trip. We arrived in Ujgorod very soon. I gave him money and headed to the station to catch my bus. While I was waiting for it and saying thank you to God for this improved situation, the worker from the station came and announced to us that our bus was one hour late. 'Oh no,' I thought to myself, It is one hour which I needed in the train and it was the reason for all my hurry. 'Oh dear. The man told me to trust God and go further, but I didn't believe him'.

I kill the hours waiting for my train on my way home.

It was a lesson for me how to trust God and listen and watch for his signs. I smiled and looked at the sky. I had a feeling that someone smiled back at me.

After twelve exhausting hours on the bus, eventually, I arrived at our Austrian house to my beloved children and husband. As I approached the house, I saw Martha who was rushing to me to greet me. She repeated the words "Gott sei

Dank," many times and kissed me passionately. Then, I came into the house and Maxim and my children greeted me with tight hugs. I was very weak standing in the hall, squeezed by their hands and I was crying from happiness.

"I'm at home … My home is here, with my family and people who love me and who I love …"

Epilogue

War Insights and a Way Forward

You do not find the happy life. You make it
—Thomas S. Monson

In Austria, my third attempt to start my life from scratch is complicated and hard. I am trying to do my little steps for the future. I have a big family. My three children need me and my strength. I must be persistent and go further to build a new future for me and my family. Also, I should think about my mission in the world, helping people, presenting them with love and happiness.

Every day, I wake up and ask myself, 'What can I do for myself, my family and for humanity?' When going to bed, I check what I've done that day.

Every day is a little but important part of our sense. We suppose that a day is just a drop in the ocean but actually, any day can change history, can make an impact on the future and make a big difference. Our days are so vital. I do not want to miss my days. I collect them like diamonds and assess their value.

The war has changed my life too much, but it will not destroy me. Furthermore, it has made me stronger and even lighter. It has brought me closer with my soul and to God. Through all the trials and sufferings, I have found a lot of love in my heart.

Our life before the war was just preparation for the exam. We had studied something, forgave someone, had hundreds of life lessons and maybe little tests during that period. But the war has been a serious exam for all of us.

During that exam you have not been able to study and do other habitual things as you have not had a solid foundation under your feet. We are in very strict conditions. We are examined as to how we can survive and how we can save our humanity and love. This is not just a war between Russia and Ukraine, it is also a war between light and dark. I feel this is a vital period for people all over the world, that now, we should stop our rushing all around and start appreciating what we really have. I am not talking about materialistic possessions. The war can reveal what we really own and what we should yet obtain.

Now, in Austria, I am doing my best with all my knowledge from the preparatory period: I teach English and help people with languages; I give psychological sessions for those who suffer and cannot find themself during the war; I provide photo sessions and make people happy; I read my books and inspire people; I do massages and speak to them, also helping their body and soul. Also, I write my poems to inspire the Austrian people around me and I have written this book to inspire as many people as possible in the world, hopefully, including you. I am doing everything that I can do in order to make this world better. It is not such an easy job as God sometimes sends me hard periods to make me think deeper and find more sense in my way, to stop my ego and teach me love.

What vital knowledge have I learned because of the war?

Saving our love and humanity must always be top priority - Wars provoke us to hate and curse our enemies but we must remember that hate can never beat hate. Only love can beat it. If we fall into hatred, we lose our humanity and our soul. It would be easy to hate the Russians, but I do not feel hatred. I have love and God in my heart. It was a harsh fight in my soul, but I am happy that light has won.

All your possessions are temporary - We buy things in order to enjoy our life and to make ourselves happier not to keep them until some future appropriate moment. You must believe that the moment is now. Use your possessions, put on your favourite clothes, eat the most delicious food and get enjoyment when you can and until you can.

Your current bad period in life may not be the worst - Perhaps, you are mistaken and things you thought were bad were not so bad. Bad times may be easier than you think. You might miss the chance to do a lot of things to improve your life by making the wrong conclusions on what you perceive to be bad.

I remember the time before the war. I was depressed after my grandmother's death. I lost my confidence but was trying my best to come back to normal life. Fortunately, I overcame all the obstacles. And when the war came, I realized that those days had been so happy compared to the war time.

So, try your best to achieve your goals now and don't wait for an easier period.

Love and express your love - Our life can end at any time and you can lose the opportunity to say, "I love you!" to the people who are important to you. Now, you have time to hug your kids, to share your experience with them.

During the war, a lot of children became orphans. The war took away their parental support and the foundation that such support provided. They would not receive their parents' love, support or wise words for their future.

So, don't miss the time with your children, with your husband or wife, with your parents, your friends and all other people who you consider to be crucial parts of your life.

Never postpone anything for the future. Live now! - My experience shows that life can change dramatically at any time. When I was in Ukraine, I had all the appropriate conditions for studying, developing myself, realizing my dreams and achieving my goals. All the possibilities were close at hand. I could make an effort and start doing whatever I wanted. Now in Austria, I have to fight every day in order to prove that I am worth working in the country with the same rights. I have to study German to express my thoughts and desires. I have to work hard to save money for rent and survive in a new environment.

So, take your possibilities while you are living in your country and you are its citizen, while you have rights to express your requirements and while you are young enough with the motivation and energy to act.

It is never late to start from scratch - Oh, this one is my favourite! When I had to start my life again in Kharkiv when the Russians came, back in 2014, I thought, 'Kate, at twenty-seven, you are not so young, but try to work hard and prove that you managed to achieve your goals'. It took me a lot of years of tough days and sleepless nights until I got it. In 2020, I bumped into the same problem in Austria by which time, I was almost forty, with three children, trying to move forward step by step to achieve success. After such an experience of starting from scratch, I am not afraid of anything or anyone.

Your home is the whole planet - If you have to leave your birthplace, it does not matter. It does not mean that you lose an opportunity to realize your life mission. It just means you are needed in another place and another place is better for you at that moment. You can learn a new language and keep doing what you used to do in your motherland, with the same passion and dedication. Or maybe, it is your best chance to change your life dramatically and at last, you can do what you have always dreamt about.

Be proud of your country. If you do not like something in it, change it! - When Ukrainian refugees started living in foreign countries, they found out that their country was much better than many other places in the world. We missed our developed infrastructure, good services, a wonderful banking system and a lot of other life benefits. In Ukraine, we had everything online. All our questions had been solved quickly and effectively. Before the war, we certainly had been living happily and were satisfied. But a lot of people did not appreciate this situation. Every time, they cursed the government or city establishments. Now, our reality shows that there is nothing better than our land. It was chosen for us perfectly and we should not find problems living in our country but we should try to invest our time, money, energy in its future. After the war, Ukrainians are going to come back and rebuild the country from scratch. Because of the war, they have seen its beauty, uniqueness and excellence.

I am a patriot of my country. I consider Ukraine to be the best country in the world. It is a paradise, where everything is charming: nature, people, architecture, climate, air, language. I dream about its victory. I am waiting for its victory. Afterwards, we will be prouder of our country and our nation.

Squeeze your lemon as much as you can and prepare something delicious - In Austria, initially, I was restricted. It was a new place with new challenges and initially, no foundation and financial background for me. I felt that my life was like a lemon. It was sour and terrible. I was offered a job as an English teacher at a school but later, I was rejected as I needed to have B2 level of German. I was thinking of becoming a photographer, but Austrian people were not so fond of photos like in Ukraine. I tried to do a lot of deals. I did not want to give up. I kept squeezing my lemon more and more to make more and more dishes. My challenging conditions provoked me to come up with new ideas and plans. I was persistently trying to find the best recipe for me even with a lemon taste. Writing this book is one of my attempts to prepare something delicious and at the same time, I hope, something important for the world.

Nothing is over until it is actually over - The war is the worst thing ever. It grabs everything you have and leaves you broke and lonely.

Millions of Ukrainians have lost their family, their kids, their homes, work, stability and hopes for the future. I saw a man who came home after work and found that his house was destroyed. He had lost his wife, his mother and his twin two-year-old daughters. He said, "I do not see a sense in living any further. I do not have any desire to live!"

People now find themselves alone, penniless and in despair. They see no way forward. I understand and sympathise with them. I cannot imagine what I would have felt if I had lost my children or my husband. But I am confident that they must live and continue giving their light. Everything is possible for reconstruction. It takes a lot of time and effort but it is worth trying. We have such trials which we can endure. Our souls wanted us to go through all these hurdles and losses.

Personally, I lost my houses several times, I lost the opportunity to see my parents for eight years, I could not see my beloved grandmother and grandfather before their deaths. I lost my business which I had been building brick by brick for more than ten years. But I am not going to give up. It is not the end of my life. I am still alive, so I can find new ways to be happy again. I am very tired but not conquered.

Our wealth is our family, our resource is our brain - The war showed me that I could survive and overcome everything if my family is next to me. They are my inspiration and my power. They inspire me to act and move. They gave me light when it was darkness.

I remember the day when my daughter Annya said in Austria, "Mum, you are the best mother. You do so much for us, you work hard and look after us. But you are so tired sometimes. Find time to have a rest and I can help you." My son Misha also came to me and asked, "Mum, maybe, you need my help?" My husband did his best every day to make my life easier and quieter. And my little Lev simply came to me and hugged me a hundred times a day, kissing my face and saying, "I love you." Having all this treasure, I cannot give up. I do not have the right to stop.

My brain helped me to learn new languages, to acquire new knowledge, to get a new job and, of course, to start writing this book.

Money and possessions are not stable. But if you have a loving family and an ability to study again and again, you can achieve everything. Be persistent and determined. And remember, no obstacles are ever insurmountable.

I wanted to finish my book with a happy end.

I hope to find a new house and start living without fear, get a stable job, and send my children to local schools speaking German fluently. I want to write books and perform around the world in front of thousands of people, speaking about love, happiness, and the purpose of life. This is a list of my dreams which I want to come true. But I understand that reality cannot come quickly. I know that for this, I will have to work extremely hard to claw my life back to success. It is a long way back but I am ready for it. I will not hesitate doing God's work and I will always be dedicated to my mission. The war gave me this unspeakably strong will to help people.

I will take on this responsibility.

Appendix

Important Poems

A selection taken from my performance in Austria.

Thank you, God
God, thank you for this newly day.
For the sunrise and rays of blessing.
Thank you that you are on my way.
And I can feel your love and caring.

Thanks for the people in my life,
Who make me smile and wipe my tears.
Who can protect and give advice,
Who mention me in their prayers.
Who can inspire for the changes,
And always trust me and support.
God, Thank you for these holy angels,
You always give me what I want.
And thanks for those who hurt me deeply,
They made me strong and taught me love.
You are the one who knows exactly,
What obstacles I should revive.

God, thank you for your daily presents,
I am keeping faith in all you give.
You are enriching my life essence,
I always love you and believe!

How nice!
How nice! My kids are sleeping in the beds,
The house is fine and loving man is near.
I always can call either parents or my friends.
And in my city there's tranquil atmosphere.
How nice! I am able to reach any goals,
I've got a rain of chances every morning.
And I can choose at ease my social roles.
The world presents me knowledge for exploring.
How nice! My work reflects my needs of soul,
There is enough finance for daily wishes.
My life is fortunate and happy in the whole.
Experience gives sense and every day enriches.
How nice! I am living now in certain place,
At this specific time and in the given body.
I am grateful for each present on my race,
I am writing my unique and honest story.

If you need light
Look at your life from brighter side.
And in the dark light up yourself.
The world is generous and kind.
And gives you all the sky's upheld.
To clean your soul to gloss of pure.
And you will see the other life.
It will be happy and secure,
It will reflect your world inside.
The more light you are shining out,
The more you're sending gratis love,
You'll get sky's gifts in large amount,
And always get help from above.

Fly up me dear
My dear, always listen to your inner voice,
And go until you reach your happy valleys.
Take care of love, it should affect your choice.
Your heart and soul must be your constant allies.

Don't be afraid to seek, reveal your gift.
The world will always wait and need in you.
Fly up to cherished dream instead exist.
And long-awaited rise is coming into view.

People angels
There are people you're inspired by,
With whom you want to talk about life,
Who make you smile and stop your cry,
You're filled with bliss, when they arrive.
They are Earth angels with an open heart,
They always come for healing people's souls.
And next to them you feel that you heat up.
And you are eager to reach any goals.
They wander among us and sparkle world,
And gently touching those who pray at night.
And fill your thoughts with kind and helpful word,
And all the things fall into places right.
Believe, these people – angels are throughout.
God sends us help through their caring hands.
Your angel's near you, without doubt,
And waiting for your genuine commands.

What is your life about?
What is your life about? Tell me now.
Is there lots of love and happy moments?
What do you give yourself and what allow?
How often do you have your soul performance?
How often have you cheated and been lied?
How many losses, pain and tears?
What do you take from people? What provide?
And do you often thank God in your prayers?
How quickly are your years going past?
And do you have stops in your journey?
Do you have anybody you can trust?
Or do you waste your time in worrying?
And are the months filled of your joy?
And how much luck is there on your way?
Do you obtain the gifts or just avoid?
Follow the heart's voice or obey?
What are your weeks about? What's your part?
How much routine and chores do you fill in?
What do you see behind and what in front?
And are you sure that it is your dream?
What are your days about? What's in this?
What vital thing have you already done?
And have you managed to find major keys?
A little more and your day will be gone.
What can the hours say about you?
What do they strike about and for whom?
Can you confirm that you are always true?
Is it enough love in your soul room?
What is this moment like? And are you in?
Where is your focus and your thoughts?
This moment is unique you've ever been,
Begin your new life from the basic course.

Appreciate your days
Appreciate the day within the family.
It's like a postcard sent from heavens.
You've got a chance to spend these hours happily.
Enjoy the time with them, filling impressions.
Hold your kid's hands and hug them frequently,
Because there's nothing more significant in life.
Keep any moment, striking balance equally.
They're growing fast, don't waste the precious time.
To celebrate each day among the family,
And value time presented lavishly by God.
Don't drown in sadness, pain and vanity.
It's high time to change purpose and restart.

Ukraine, go ahead!
Ukraine is a place of love and freedom,
It is my motherland, my paradise.
I walk along its streets like in museum,
And striking sightseeing is in front of eyes.
It is a promised land with open people,
It is the prettiest spot on the whole Earth.
And opportunities for everyone are equal,
If you work hard, you always get your goals.
Ukraine is a country for the journeys.
There are a lot of rivers, lakes and seas.
It is rich in its valleys, parks and forests.
And here you can always freely breathe.
I am happy that Ukraine was my birthplace.
It is an honour living on its land.
And soon I will come back to my home doorstep.
Please, don't give up, my country, go ahead!

A way of the soul
In the sky angels are so excited
They are sending a soul to the Earth.
A good body for it is provided.
It has got a new chance for a birth.
It is landing on the ground slowly.
Magic world is awaiting ahead.
It is light with no fear and worrying.
The soul knows how the days will be spent.
The boy screamed about his coming,
And he opened his angelic eyes.
Everyone was kissing and hugging.
"Did you wait for me? I am your surprise!"
He grew up every year so quickly.
Lots of people were trying to teach.
He was limited and brought up strictly.
In the cage he could barely breathe.
But the soul is unwilling to listen.
Money, fashion is not its main goal.
It is hard to have this tough condition.
People change its significant role.
It was dreaming about the different
It planned doing the sensible things.
Our life is so fast and momentary,
We can't miss all the chances it gives.
Earthly time is passing non-stoppable.
Work and family, duties and dog …
Everything' going wrong and improperly.
The soul's dream is hidden in fog.
It is waiting for time of revealing,
Life is boring if you just exist.
There are lots of things to exploring,
The soul has an extensive wish list.

It would like to answer the questions:
What is love and who is your friend?
How to go through life difficult lessons,
And stay happy and kind in the end?
How can you realize your main purpose?
Be assertive to goals and stay wise?
How to find out the heavenly service?
Save your light and avoid stars in eyes.
Ageing has come to his lonely doorstep,
Most of life's inevitably gone.
He's become very weak running non-stop,
He remembered the list wasn't done.
And he says sadly: My soul, come here.
Tell me what chance in life I have lost.
I was driving so fast, changing gear,
I regret I had missed vital stops.
Soon my life will be striking the finish,
And I will have to fly to the skies.
Sorry, soul, your hopes were diminished.
I was deaf to your hearty replies.

***

In the sky the soul is being greeted
Angels ask: Have you served your main sense?
The soul nodded and sadly admitted.
"No, unfortunately I've lost my chance ..."

The happiest day
I can do everything I want.
Today I really like myself.
I am capable to change the world.
And all my problems will be delt.
My will is stronger every day!
I am full of energy and force.
I always get luck on my way,
Today I will make a right choice.
I'm not afraid to make a challenge.
My soul will guide me to success.
Today's my chance to gift my talent,
In all my plans I will progress.
My deeds are truly filled with passion!
I'm fond of everything I do.
My life is full of satisfaction ,
I always find out something new.
My purpose for this world is vital,
I'm a key part in human's chains.
Today I'll paint my life far brighter.
It is one of my happiest days!

God helps us through other people
God always helps through other people,
He sends us angels on the way.
And when we are falling from the steep hill
These people give a hoping ray.
They're always ready to support all.
They don't pretend and always smile.
And their role is so important,
As good deals make the world fertile.